THE M. & E. HANDBOOK SERIES

AN OUTLINE OF MONETARY THEORY

J. L. HANSON,
M.A., M.Ed. (Leeds), Ph.D., B.Sc.(Econ.) London
Formerly Senior Lecturer in charge of Economics, Huddersfield College of Technology (now Huddersfield Polytechnic)

THIRD EDITION

MACDONALD AND EVANS

MACDONALD & EVANS LTD.
8 John Street, London WC1N 2HY

First published February 1966
Reprinted July 1967
Reprinted July 1968
Reprinted August 1969
Second Edition September 1971
Reprinted January 1973
Reprinted (with amendments) April 1974
Third Edition March 1976

ISBN: 0 7121 1521 8

Printed in Great Britain by
Lowe & Brydone (Printers) Ltd., Thetford, Norfolk

PREFACE TO THE THIRD EDITION

This book is intended for students who are preparing for specific examinations in monetary theory and also for those who are studying for examinations in economics which include this branch of the subject. Thus, Part I provides a survey of the working of the British monetary system today; Part II covers international monetary relations; Part III deals with matters arising from the dynamic aspect of money, that is, problems associated with changes in the value of money, saving and investment, and the aims and methods of monetary policy; and the final section, Part IV, is devoted to monetary problems of the present day.

The subject-matter is presented in the form of study notes. Monetary theory, however, cannot be seriously studied from a mere outline of the subject. A knowledge of the bare minimum necessary to scrape through an examination is of little value to anyone and soon forgotten. An intellectual study such as monetary theory must of necessity comprise primarily a training in a particular line of thinking and not merely the memorising of facts, which in any case are liable to change. The purpose of this book, therefore, is not to enable a student to avoid the wider reading which a study of this subject entails, but to supplement it.

Its aim is threefold. (1) In all branches of economics, including monetary theory, it is often difficult for those beginning their studies to see the wood for the trees, so that a quick survey of the whole field provides a useful introduction and prepares the way to a better understanding of the topics that confront them in the early part of the course. (2) If it is used alongside a more detailed reading of the subject it should assist the student more fully to understand each topic as it arises. This book should prove very useful for both these purposes. (3) Its third aim is to provide the student with a comprehensive set of notes to enable him, when he has completed his study of each section of the subject, to revise his work without risk of his perpetuating the errors which almost inevitably tend to creep into his own notes. To make one's own notes is a most valuable exercise and a practice to be strongly recommended since their compilation compels the student to clarify his ideas, but the use of such notes may have serious consequences if revision is based entirely on them. This book, therefore, aims to provide the student with a reliable set of notes for revision purposes. To conform with other volumes in the series there is appended to each part of the book a test which the student is advised to use as a means of assessing his progress.

For the present edition the book has been thoroughly revised to take account of recent changes and developments in monetary practice. The opportunity has been taken to bring the statistics up-to-date.

June 1975 J. L. H.

NOTICE TO LECTURERS

Many lecturers are now using **HANDBOOKS** as working texts to save time otherwise wasted by students in protracted note-taking. The purpose of the series is to meet practical teaching requirements as far as possible, and lecturers are cordially invited to forward comments or criticisms to the publishers for consideration.

P. W. D. REDMOND *General Editor*

CONTENTS

PART ONE:

A SURVEY OF THE BRITISH MONETARY SYSTEM

CHAPTER I

THE ORIGIN AND FUNCTIONS OF MONEY

THE ORIGIN OF MONEY

1. The importance of money.

(a) A complex modern economic system could not function efficiently without it.

(b) Under modern methods of large-scale production each employee undertakes only a single process, so that he has to rely on others to supply his wants. This necessitates the use of a medium of exchange.

(c) Both production and distribution are simplified if, for their services to production, people are paid money wages.

2. Money-less economies. Some economies in the past functioned with little or no money:

(a) Under the medieval manorial system villeins paid rent for their land by working for the lord, and freemen paid rent in kind.

(b) The Incas of Peru are said to have managed without money, both production and distribution being fully controlled by the State.

3. Barter. This is the exchange of goods for goods. Drawbacks to barter were:

(a) Before a transaction could take place two people had to be brought together each of whom could offer the other something he wanted.
(b) A rate of exchange between the goods concerned had to be agreed upon.
(c) It was difficult to exchange large for small or "dear" for "cheap" commodities.

4. A medium of exchange. This is something not wanted for its own sake and used only to facilitate exchange. Money probably first came into use as a medium of exchange.

FROM COMMODITY MONEY TO BANKNOTES

5. Commodity money.

(a) Commodities that were generally acceptable came to be employed as money.

(b) Such commodities had to be valuable for their own sake, either for use or ornament.

Examples of commodity money: cowrie shells, cattle, sheep, tea, salt, sugar, tobacco, iron, silver, gold.

6. Qualities of a good medium of exchange.

(a) It must be generally acceptable.
(b) It should not be too bulky.
(c) It should be capable of being easily carried about.
(d) It should be easily divisible into fractional units.
(e) It should be homogeneous in character.
(f) It should be fairly durable.
(g) It should be scarce but not too scarce.

7. Development of coinage.

(a) The precious metals soon superseded other media of exchange, merchants weighing out quantities of metal as required.

(b) Merchants began to carry with them pieces of metal of a known weight.

(c) Coins of a known weight and fineness of metal came to be minted, but these continued to be weighed whenever their quality was doubted.

8. Development of paper money.

(a) The London goldsmiths gave receipts to merchants who deposited coin with them for safe-keeping.

(b) The goldsmiths issued receipts in convenient denominations.

(c) The goldsmiths became bankers and their receipts then

served as convertible banknotes exchangeable on demand for coin.

(d) Inconvertible paper money was issued during 1797–1821, during 1919–26 and since 1931 (during 1926–31 notes were exchangeable only for gold bars weighing 400 oz.). Only comparatively recently, therefore, have inconvertible banknotes become generally accepted as money.

9. Advantages and disadvantages of inconvertible banknotes.

(a) Advantages: If generally acceptable they possess all the qualities of a good medium of exchange (*see* **6** above).

(b) Disadvantages: There is no physical limitation on the issue of inconvertible paper money. Since 1844 a number of Acts of Parliament (1844, 1928, 1954) have placed restrictions on the fiduciary issue (*see* IV, **4**).

BANK DEPOSITS AS MONEY

10. Cheques and bank deposits. A cheque is a written order by the drawer to the banker to pay a specified sum to some other person. It is merely a means by which bank deposits are transferred from one person's account to another's.

Although the cheque has become the principal means of payment in some countries it is the bank deposit and not the cheque that is to be regarded as money.

Thus, the bank deposit is the final stage in the development of money.

11. Acceptability of cheques. A cheque is not generally acceptable. Nor is it legal tender. It is only of value if the drawer has a sufficient bank balance to meet it.

12. The volume of bank deposits. When calculating the total volume of bank deposits it has been usual in the past to add together the total deposits of the commercial banks on current and deposit account, but to exclude deposits with savings banks.

For some time, however, the National Savings Bank* has permitted its customers to draw cheques, and since 1965 the Trustee Savings Bank has been allowed to offer current accounts to their customers. To some extent, therefore, a portion of the ordinary deposits of the savings banks, and possibly also deposits in building societies serve, like the

*Formerly the Post Office Savings Bank.

balances on deposit account of the commercial banks, as reserves of purchasing power.

Thus, the total amount of money in the form of bank deposits is now rather more than the total deposits of the commercial banks.

SOME ASPECTS OF MONEY

13. Money and the State. The State has attempted to exercise control over the various kinds of money in the following ways:

(a) The minting of coins. At an early date the minting of coins came to be regarded as a State privilege. The State also decided the metallic content of the coins.

(b) The issue of banknotes. The Acts of 1844, 1928 and 1954 controlled the issue of banknotes in England.

(c) The volume of bank deposits. Through its monetary policy the State can influence the volume of bank deposits.

14. Legal tender.

(a) Money is full legal tender when the State declares that it can be used for the payment of debts up to any amount, *e.g.* Bank of England notes in England.

(b) Token coins are limited legal tender only up to specified amounts.

15. "Fiat" money. This is money authorised by the State. The State's "fiat," however, is not sufficient to make a commodity serve as money:

(a) The commodity selected for use as money must be generally acceptable.

(b) The State can however help to make "fiat" money acceptable by itself using it to make payments and accepting it in payment of taxes.

16. Gresham's Law. This term (it is hardly a law) is used of the statement that "bad money drives out good," attributed to Sir Thomas Gresham, monetary adviser to Elizabeth I.

Gresham had noticed that the debasement of the coinage under Henry VIII had this effect. When good and bad money circulate together the velocity of circulation increases for the bad money and falls for the good money.

17. Exceptions to Gresham's Law. This "law" does not appear to operate in the following circumstances:

(a) When the amount of bad money in circulation is so small that some payments have to be made in good money.

(b) If the amount in circulation is small, people may refuse to accept the bad money.

(c) If for a long time people have been accustomed to a particular coin of full face value they may continue to accept it even though it becomes very worn and obviously below weight.

18. Bi-metallism. This occurs when two metallic standards are in force at the same time so that, for example, both gold and silver coins of full face value are minted.

(a) Advantages of bi-metallism.

(i) It provides a currency of more stable value;

(ii) It would facilitate exchange between areas on the gold standard and those on a silver standard. Neither of these points is, however, of importance today.

(b) Disadvantages. It could function only if there was a constant ratio between the prices of the two metals—an impossible condition. During the past hundred years, for example, gold has increased in value relatively to silver by more than three times. If one metal became more valuable in terms of the other the more valuable coin, according to Gresham's Law, would be driven out of circulation.

FUNCTIONS OF MONEY

19. Money as a medium of exchange. This is probably the oldest function of money (*see* I, **4**) and other functions developed from it.

20. Money as a unit of account.

(a) Money also provided a means by which goods and services could be given *prices*, thereby saving time spent in bargaining. A unit of account too is required for economic calculations, *e.g.* the relative cost of alternative schemes of production. (To serve as a unit of account a commodity need not possess all the attributes of a good monetary medium.)

(b) This function of money is sometimes expressed in the form "money as a measure of value". But value cannot be

measured since it is subjective in character, though prices may often approximately indicate relative values. In any case money is a poor measure, as its own value is liable to change.

21. Money as a store of value. Money can be stored for spending at a later date to satisfy future wants, whereas many goods are perishable and so cannot be stored.

Money can satisfactorily fulfil this function only if:

(a) It retains its value. Over the centuries there has been a tendency for the value of money to fall. Since 1914 the value of money has fallen everywhere and in some countries catastrophically.

(b) Goods and services are available when required. The reason for this is that most goods have to be currently produced, money itself being only a *claim* to goods and services.

22. Money as a means for making deferred payments. Money makes possible credit transactions and future contracts. Thus:

(a) Business firms can borrow to finance production.
(b) Consumers can buy goods on credit.
(c) Governments can borrow by the creation of securities.

This assists real investment.

23. Money generalises purchasing power. People prefer to be paid for their services in money rather than to be paid in kind as money enables them to make their own choice among competing wants.

24. Money as a liquid asset. To hold assets in the form of money enables a person to consider his disposal of it:

(a) Whether to spend it or save it.
(b) Whether to buy something now or in the future (perhaps in the hope of a fall in price).

(c) Whether to invest it now or in the future (if he thinks the rate of interest may rise) thereby allowing him time to decide what type of investment to select.

25. Money and the price mechanism.

(a) By means of the price mechanism a heterogeneous mass of goods and services which are scarce, relative to the

demand for them, can be distributed among the huge number of people who want them.

(b) Changes in demand or in conditions of supply affect prices and through the price mechanism bring demand and supply into equilibrium again.

(c) No elaborate machinery is required for the working of the price mechanism, but money is necessary in order to be able to assign prices to goods and services. This is an important function of money in a free economy.

26. Money as a dynamic force. These are all passive, static or technical functions of money. Only fairly recently has it been realised that money can also have a dynamic function, that is, that changes in the supply of money can influence the level of economic activity and employment. This function of money is considered in Part Three of this book.

CHAPTER II

THE COMMERCIAL BANKS AND THE SUPPLY OF MONEY

DEVELOPMENT OF COMMERCIAL BANKING

1. Money-changers. The earliest banking activity was that of money-changing. Banking in Europe developed first in Italy, Venice and other cities having banks in the Middle Ages.

2. The Goldsmiths.

(a) The earliest bankers in England were the London goldsmiths, Having facilities for the storage of valuables they began to accept deposits of money for safe-keeping in the early seventeenth century as a sideline to their ordinary business.

(b) From the goldsmiths' receipts the *banknote* developed.

(c) They further developed their banking business by lending to the king, the nobility and others, generally at very high rates of interest.

3. Development of private banking.

(a) Towards the end of the seventeenth century banking had increased, to such an extent that it could no longer be combined with the business of a goldsmith.

(b) The earliest private banks were "hived off" from goldsmiths' businesses and almost all were situated in London.

(c) Country private banks came into being with the Industrial Revolution, generally as offshoots of the businesses of merchants and manufacturers.

(d) Country banks increased from a total of twelve in 1750 to 781 by 1821.

4. Joint-stock banks.

(a) Founded in 1694, the Bank of England was for 132 years the only joint-stock bank in England.

(b) Not until 1826 were any more joint-stock banks allowed to be established in England and only then provided they were outside a radius of 65 miles from London.

(c) After 1833 joint-stock banks were permitted in London if they did not issue banknotes.

5. Expansion and amalgamation of banks. The weakness of private banks in times of crisis assisted the expansion of joint-stock banking. The joint-stock banks expanded by:

(a) Opening new branches.
(b) Amalgamating with private banks.
(c) Amalgamating with one another.

As a result, by 1913 the number of banks in England fell to 97, of which 60 were private banks. In consequence of further amalgamations, the present "Big Four" were created—the Midland, Barclays, Lloyds, the National Westminster.

6. Branch banking. A main feature of British banking is the existence of four very large commercial banks each with a large number of branches distributed throughout the whole country. Such banks have proved themselves better able to withstand financial crises than the unit banks found in most parts of the U.S.A.

7. Types of bank. There are four main types of bank:

(a) The central bank, the main function of which is to carry out a country's monetary policy and control the other banks, *e.g.* the Bank of England. Almost every country now has a central bank. Such banks work closely with the State (*see* III).

(b) Commercial banks. Often still known in England as joint-stock banks or nowadays more frequently as clearing banks they undertake most kinds of banking business, including the granting of credit (*see* **8-12** below).

(c) Merchant banks. Sometimes known as accepting houses, they are found mainly in the City of London. They specialise in business connected with bills of exchange, especially foreign bills, but with the decline in this means of payment they have begun to undertake an increasing amount of ordinary banking business (*see* V).

(d) Savings banks. These banks were established mainly to encourage small savers, and so have no business accounts.

Every large town in the U.K. had its trustee savings bank, but only the National Savings Bank has many branches. The *Page Report* (1973) recommended that the trustee savings banks should be given full banking status, one of the conditions being that the 73 savings banks that then existed should be merged into larger regional units—ten in England and Wales, four in Scotland and one in Northern Ireland. The first to be formed was for London and the south.

Some other institutions, generally called "financial intermediaries," accept deposits—building societies, hire purchase companies. Since 1971 some finance houses have acquired full banking status.

FUNCTIONS OF COMMERCIAL BANKS

8. Accepting deposits. Accepting deposits for safe-keeping is one of the oldest functions of British banks. At the present day, customers open deposit accounts:

(a) As a means of accumulating savings.
(b) As a reserve to supplement a current account.

Interest (usually 2 per cent below the Bank of England's minimum lending rate) is paid on deposit accounts, and generally notice of withdrawal is required.

9. Issuing banknotes. At one time most commercial banks possessed the right to issue their own banknotes. Banks in Scotland, Northern Ireland and the Isle of Man still enjoy this privilege to a limited extent, but in England only the Bank of England now has the right to issue banknotes.

10. Acting as agents of payment. The cheque makes it possible to use bank deposits as a means of payment. Cheques enable bank deposits to be transferred from one person's account to that of another. In order to pay by cheque it is necessary to open a current account. Most banks pay no interest on deposits on current account but instead charge a commission for clearing customers' cheques.

11. Lending to customers. At an early date bankers discovered that it was safe to lend some of the money deposited with them. In time they found that it was possible to lend more than this—provided they were always able to pay cash on demand to those entitled to ask for it. Banks lend in the following ways:

(a) By *overdraft*, the bank permitting the borrower to draw cheques for a period up to a maximum agreed sum in excess of the amount standing to his credit in his current account. Interest is payable only on the amount by which the account is overdrawn.

(b) By the *loan* of a fixed sum for a definite period. "Personal loans" to cover the purchase of expensive goods are of this type. Interest in this case is payable on the entire loan.

(c) By *discounting bills of exchange*, thereby enabling the debtor to postpone payment and the creditor to be paid promptly.

(d) By *financing hire-purchase* transactions. Since 1958 all the English commercial banks have had hire-purchase finance companies as subsidiaries

12. Agents for customers. Banks act as agents for their customers in the purchase or sale of stock exchange securities, the issue of travellers' cheques and bank drafts, foreign exchange business, acting as trustees or executors, or providing a reference for a customer, etc.

THE IMPORTANCE OF BANK DEPOSITS

13. The volume of bank deposits. Bank deposits, subject to transfer by cheque, as already noted form the most important kind of money in use in Great Britain today (about 80% of the total money in use).

14. The creation of bank deposits. An increase in bank deposits occurs when:

(a) A payment of cash is made by a customer into his bank account, provided this is not offset by a withdrawal of cash for a similar amount.

(b) A cheque is placed by a customer to the credit of his account. In general this means that the deposits of the bank on which the cheque is drawn will be reduced by the same amount, so that the total deposits of the two banks remain unchanged. If, however, a customer has been granted an overdraft by his bank he can draw cheques in excess of the amount standing to his credit, and such cheques increase the

deposits of the payee's bank without reducing the deposits of the drawer's bank, thereby increasing total bank deposits.

(c) A bank purchases Government securities—Treasury bills or Government stocks—in order to increase its investments. This is equivalent to the bank lending to the Government, the bank paying for its purchase by a cheque drawn on itself.

Thus bank loans create bank deposits.

The following table shows how bank deposits have increased in recent years:

Date	*Total deposits*
	£ million
1938	1,244
1945	4,692
1950	6,068
1955	6,460
1960	7,208
1965	8,397
1970	10,469
1975	22,785

15. Limitations on the creation of deposits by banks. The power of the commercial banks to create deposits is limited in the following ways:

(a) The banks must keep in line in credit expansion. Each of the commercial banks maintains a balance at the Bank of England, and these balances are used to settle indebtedness between banks arising from the clearing of cheques. Over a period of time these settlements cancel out, but if one bank adopted a more extensive credit policy than the other banks it would suffer a persistent drain on its reserves at the Bank of England (which it regards as cash), and this would compel it to reverse its policy.

(b) The liquidity rules of the banks. To meet demands of its customers for cash a bank must maintain a reserve of cash. Experience has taught English banks that this requires them to maintain a ratio of 8 per cent between their cash and total deposits. *A second liquidity ratio of 28 per cent* (for a long time 30 per cent was the recognised ratio) also existed between the more liquid assets—cash, money at call, bills discounted—and deposits. Since a bank which is short of cash could easily call

in money at call in order to restore its 8 per cent cash ratio, it was this second liquidity ratio of 28 per cent that became the more important. In 1971 the Bank of England suggested a new liquidity rule: cash, money at call, Treasury bills and a proportion of commercial bills and Government stocks within one year of maturity should form 12½ per cent of a bank's assets. Thus, an increase in a bank's lending is dependent on its increasing its cash reserves.

(c) The supply of collateral security. To the extent that banks require borrowers to put up collateral security against loans this acts as a further restriction on their power to grant credit. It is not a very effective check on their credit policy, since the supply of such security depends largely on the banks' standards. Further, banks often lend on the security of a borrower's good name.

THE BALANCE SHEET OF A BANK

16. The more liquid assets of a commercial bank. A glance at the balance sheet on page 14 will show that these comprise:

(a) Coin, notes and balance with the Bank of England. This is a commercial bank's cash reserve and, therefore, its most liquid asset. The coin and notes are distributed among the various branches. The balance at the Bank of England, on which no interest is paid, is regarded as cash, since withdrawals in cash can be made from it.

(b) Money at call and short notice. This represents a bank's lending to the members of the money market (*see* V).

(c) Bills discounted. In 1971 about 40% of the bills discounted by the English commercial banks were Treasury bills.

17. The less liquid assets of a commercial bank. These comprise:

(a) Special deposits. As an instrument of monetary policy (*see* IV, 10) these were first employed in 1960. The Bank of England can demand special deposits from the commercial banks (a stated percentage of their ordinary deposits) in order to reduce their cash reserves and so curtail their lending. Interest is paid on special deposits, in contrast to the ordinary balances of the commercial banks, which are interest-free.

(b) Investments. These are mainly in British Government

The combined balance sheets of the London clearing banks
(only the more important items are shown)

	1970	1975
	£ million	£ million
Assets		
Coin, notes and balances with Bank of England	865	976
Money at call and short notice	1,556	1,181
Bills discounted		
Treasury bills	207	400
Other bills	714	726
Special deposits	366	554
Investments	1,069	1,260
Advances to customers	5,737	13,242
Liabilities		
Deposits	10,469	22,785

stocks, generally those within five years of their redemption date.

(c) Advances to customers. This asset, the most profitable asset of a commercial bank, tends to vary inversely with investments, a bank increasing its advances and reducing its investments at times of strong business activity. Advances—mainly for the provision of working capital—are made to agriculture, to all kinds of manufacturing industry, to commercial undertakings, and to financial institutions and professional people. Advances also include personal loans.

18. The structure of a bank's balance sheet. The balance sheet of a bank exemplifies very clearly the "banker's dilemma"—the reconciliation of his concern for the liquidity of his assets and his desire to increase his profit, since the more profitable an asset the less liquid it is likely to be. Hence, the second liquidity rule of the English commercial banks: to hold their more liquid assets at a minimum of $12\frac{1}{2}$ per cent of their deposits.

19. Recent changes in the banks' balance sheets. The following are the most important changes that have taken place in the combined balance sheets of the London clearing banks in recent years:

(a) The huge increase in bank deposits, especially during the 1970s when the total more than doubled in four years.

(b) The cash ratio was reduced in 1946, at the request of the Bank of England, from 10 per cent to 8 per cent.

(c) The ratio of the more liquid assets to deposits was reduced from 30 per cent to 28 per cent in 1964.

(d) The Bank of England introduced a new liquidity rule of 12½ per cent in 1971.

(e) With the increase in bank lending the ratio of investments to advances has fallen very considerably in recent years, especially since 1960—from 40 per cent in that year to 9½ per cent in 1971.

(f) The introduction of special deposits, though a fairly small fraction of a bank's total assets, added a new item to the balance sheet in 1960.

CHAPTER III

THE DEVELOPMENT AND FUNCTIONS OF THE BANK OF ENGLAND

FOUNDATION OF THE BANK OF ENGLAND

1. Origin of the Bank of England. The Bank of England was founded in 1694. Although for a long time in no sense a central bank, the Bank of England differed in many ways from the other English banks:

(a) It was founded for the purpose of lending money to the king—William III—and it managed the Government's account.

(b) It was the first joint-stock bank to be established in England and, until 1826 (*see* II, **4**), it had a monopoly of joint-stock banking in Great Britain.

(c) It had a much larger capital than any of the other banks.

(d) It was the only bank at the time with *limited liability,* other banks having to wait till 1858 for this privilege.

2. Prestige of the Bank of England. For the reasons given in **1** above the Bank of England enjoyed greater prestige than the other English banks.

For over a hundred years, however, its main concern was with ordinary banking business. Only gradually during the nineteenth century did it develop into a central bank with control over the other banks.

DEVELOPMENT OF CENTRAL BANKING

3. The Currency and Banking Schools. The bank failures of 1825 and 1837 led to demands for State intervention to regulate banking, especially the issue of banknotes. There were two schools of thought:

(a) The Currency School, whose supporters believed that the note issue of every bank should be fully backed by gold, or nearly so.

(b) The Banking School, those who favoured a more flexible note issue that could be expanded whenever

necessary to meet the needs of business.

The Government inclined towards the views of the currency school and the Act of 1844 was the result.

4. The Bank Charter Act 1844. The chief provisions of this Act were:

(a) Apart from a fiduciary issue of £14 million, the note issue of the Bank of England was to be fully backed by gold or silver, provided that silver formed no more than 20 per cent of the backing.

(b) The note issues of the other 72 note-issuing banks were to be restricted to their circulation immediately prior to the passing of the Act.

(c) No other banks were to issue notes.

(d) A note-issuing bank, on opening a branch in London or amalgamating with another bank, was to lose its right to issue notes.

(e) Whenever a bank lost its right to issue notes the Bank of England was to be allowed to increase its fiduciary issue, but only by two-thirds of the amount of the lapsed issue.

(f) The work of the Bank of England was to be divided into two departments—the Issue Department and the Banking Department—with separate balance sheets to be published in a weekly Bank return (*see* **6-11,** below).

As a result of this Act the Bank of England eventually (by 1921) became the sole bank of issue in England.

5. The Bank of England as "lender of last resort."

(a) In 1825 there were many bank failures as a result of excessive lending, but no action was taken by the Bank of England.

(b) In 1837 another batch of bank failures occurred and the Bank of England for the first time acted as "lender of last resort." This is now regarded as an essential function of a central bank.

6. The Bank of England and the crises of 1847 and 1856. By the second half of the nineteenth century the Bank of England had become a central bank:

(a) In 1847 the Government encouraged the Bank of England to act as "lender of last resort" by promising to indemnify it if it exceeded the legal fiduciary issue imposed by the *Bank Charter Act* of 1844. In the event this proved to be unnecessary.

(b) In 1856 the Bank of England was again promised an Act of indemnity by the Government and in this case the note issue had to be increased beyond the legal limit.

On both occasions the Bank raised Bank rate. By the later years of the nineteenth century the Bank had become accustomed to controlling the credit policy of the commercial banks by means of variations in Bank rate and by open market operations, (*see* IV, **8**).

THE BANK RETURN: I—THE ISSUE DEPARTMENT

7. Specimen returns for the Issue Department. The following are specimen weekly returns (published every Wednesday) for the Issue Department of the Bank of England:

Liabilities

	1970	1975
	£ million	£ million
Notes issued:		
In circulation	3,416⅓	5,311
In Banking Department	39	14
Total	3,455⅓	5,325

Assets

	1970	1975
	£ million	£ million
Government debt	11	11
Government securities	3,355	5,072
Other securities	88	241
Coin (other than gold)	1	1
Fiduciary issue	3,455	5,325
Gold coin and bullion*	⅓	—
Total	3,455⅓	5,325

*Since 1971 the Bank of England has held no gold coin or bullion.

8. The liabilities and assets of the Issue Department.

(a) Liabilities. These consist entirely of the Bank of England's issue of banknotes, notes in circulation together

with the notes held in reserve in the Banking Department.

(b) Assets

(i) Government debt—direct loans made during its early years by the Bank to the Government.

(ii) Government securities—the principal asset, comprising treasury bills and Government stocks.

(iii) Other securities—mainly stocks issued by Commonwealth Governments.

(iv) Gold coin and bullion—during 1928–39 more than 60 per cent of the note issue was backed by gold. From 1939 to 1970 a small amount of gold was held by the Issue Department, but since then the country's stock of gold has been held by the Exchange Equalisation Account.

Items *(i)* to *(iii)* above provide the backing for the fiduciary issue.

THE BANK RETURN:
II—THE BANKING DEPARTMENT

9. Specimen returns for the Banking Department. The following are specimen weekly returns for the Banking Department of the Bank of England:

Liabilities

	1970	1975
	£ million	£ million
Proprietors' capital	14½	14½
Rest	3	3½
Public deposits	13	17
Special deposits	269	934
Other deposits:		
Bankers' deposits	175½	210
Other accounts	150	553
Total	625	1,732

Assets

	1970	1975
	£ million	£ million
Government securities	475	1,257
Discounts and advances	49	299
Other securities	61	161
Notes	39	14
Coin	1	1
Total	625	1,732

10. The liabilities of the Banking Department.

(a) Proprietors' capital. The capital originally subscribed by the Bank's stockholders when it was founded. When the Bank was nationalised in 1946 the stockholders received Government stock as compensation.

(b) Rest. The Bank of England's reserve.

(c) Public deposits. The amount standing to the credit of the Government's account at the Bank of England. Receipts from taxes are paid into this account and withdrawals are made to cover Government expenditure.

(d) Other deposits: bankers' deposits. The commercial banks also maintain accounts at the Bank of England:

(i) to settle indebtedness between banks arising mainly as a result of the clearing of cheques.

(ii) as a reserve to meet any heavy demands of their customers for cash, as in December and July.

These balances, therefore, form part of the cash reserves of the commercial banks.

(e) Other deposits: other accounts.

(i) The balances of Commonwealth and many foreign banks; and
(ii) The balances of the ordinary customers of the Bank of England.

(f) Special deposits. *See* II, **17.**

11. The assets of the Banking Department.

(a) Government securities.

(i) Government bonds and Treasury bills which the Bank of England has acquired directly.
(ii) "Ways and means" advances (direct lending to the Treasury).

(b) Discounts and advances. Mainly bills of exchange (mostly Treasury bills) obtained by the Bank of England from members of the money market by re-discounting bills in its capacity of "lender of last resort," together with the amount lent to the money market with bills or Government bonds as collateral security.

(c) Other securities. Bonds obtained by the Bank of England on its own initiative (in contrast to asset *(b)* above), and comprising not only Commonwealth and foreign Government stocks but also holdings in such undertakings as Finance for Industry (*see* V, **12**) and the Banker's Industrial Development Company. This is the asset that varies whenever the Bank of England makes use of "open-market operations"

as an instrument of monetary policy (*see* IV, **8**).

(d) Notes. The Bank of England's reserve of notes.

(e) Gold and silver coin. Since gold coins were withdrawn from circulation this asset has consisted mainly of silver coins, purchased from the Royal Mint, to meet the demand of the commercial banks.

THE WORK OF THE BANK OF ENGLAND

12. The functions of the Bank of England. The analysis of the weekly return of the Bank of England above gives an indication of the Bank's main functions. These can be summarised as follows:

(a) It is now the only English Bank with *the right to issue banknotes.*

(b) It acts as *banker to the British Government,* not only managing its account (public deposits) but also managing the National Debt, paying out the interest when due and floating new loans.

(c) It acts as *banker to the commercial banks* which maintain accounts with it. Not only does this assist the clearing of cheques but it also enables the Bank to influence the cash reserves of these banks by means of "open-market" operations.

(d) Great Britain's *gold reserves* continue to be stored at the Bank of England. Before 1932 this gold belonged to the Bank, but in that year some of it was transferred to the Exchange Equalisation Account of the Treasury. On the outbreak of war in 1939 almost the whole of the Bank's remaining stock of gold was transferred to this account. Gold is no longer required as backing for the note issue and since 1972 its importance for international settlements has declined.

(e) It acts as *"lender of last resort"* to the discount houses, the minimum rate at which the Bank will re-discount first-class or bank bills formerly being Bank rate (this function is considered more fully in Chapter V).

(f) Responsibility for monetary policy used to be one of the principal functions of a central bank. The Bank of England was solely responsible for monetary policy before 1914. During 1919–1939 it acted only after consulting the Treasury. Since 1944, however, monetary policy has been the responsibility of the Chancellor of the Exchequer working

with the Treasury and the Governor of the Bank of England. In carrying out monetary policy the Bank of England now acts simply as the Government's agent. It is through the Bank of England that the Government makes its wishes known to the commercial banks and other financial institutions (this function is considered more fully in Chapter IV).

13. Functions of a central bank. For a bank to function effectively as a central bank it is essential for it to possess means of controlling the commercial banks and to do this it must act as banker to them—*(c)* above. Functions *(e)* and *(f)* are of vital importance to a central bank. It is also an advantage to possess function *(a)*. On account of the size of the turnover of the Government's account it is better for it to be with the central bank, as otherwise it would have too disturbing an effect on the banking system. The Bank of England has few ordinary customers, ordinary banking business not being regarded as a suitable activity of a central bank.

CHAPTER IV

THE BANK OF ENGLAND AND THE SUPPLY OF MONEY

THE SUPPLY OF BANKNOTES AND COIN

1. Early note issues. In the early days of banking every bank wished to issue notes, the lending of its own notes being a very profitable activity. The development of cheques made a note issue less desirable.

Until 1795, when it issued its first £5 note, the Bank of England issued no notes for less than £10. During the Napoleonic war, when gold coins ceased to circulate, notes for £2 and £1 were issued.

2. Development of the note issue, 1797–1928.

(a) By the *Bank Restriction Act* 1797, Bank of England notes of all denominations were made legal tender, including the new £2 and £1 notes, but they were not exchangeable on demand for gold.

(b) Cash payments were resumed in 1821, that is, Bank of England notes again became convertible.

(c) An Act of 1826 permitted the establishment of joint-stock banks if located beyond a radius of 65 miles from London, and these banks were given the right to issue their own notes. The same Act prohibited the Bank of England from issuing notes for less than £5.

(d) The *Bank Charter Act* 1833, declared Bank of England notes to be legal tender up to any amount.

(e) The *Bank Charter Act* 1844, restricted the fiduciary issue of the Bank of England and the issues of all banks issuing notes (*see* III, **4**). The ultimate effect of these restrictions was to make the Bank of England by 1921 the only bank of issue in England. Long before that date the commercial banks had begun to grant overdrafts instead of lending their own notes. A number of banks in Scotland, Northern Ireland and the Isle of Man, however, retain the right to issue their own notes, but these issues are strictly regulated.

(f) Treasury notes (or currency notes) were issued by the Treasury during 1915–28, gold coins being withdrawn.

3. The Currency and Banknotes Act 1928. When gold coins were withdrawn during the First World War the Treasury issued notes for £1 and 10*s.* to replace them. These notes circulated alongside Bank of England notes for £5 and upwards. The Act of 1928 brought the entire note issue under the Bank of England, as had been recommended in 1918 by the *Cunliffe Committee:*

(a) The fiduciary issue of the Bank of England was to be *increased* to £260 million, backed by securities (or silver to a maximum of £5½ million).

(b) The Bank of England was empowered to issue notes for £1 and 10*s.* (since 1826 it had been allowed to issue notes for less than £5).

(c) All notes in excess of the fiduciary issue were to be fully backed by gold, thereby maintaining the principle laid down in the *Bank Charter Act* of 1844.

(d) Variations in the amount of the fiduciary issue must have the consent of the Treasury.

4. The fiduciary issue.

(a) The restrictions on the fiduciary issue by the *Bank Charter Act* of 1844 were to prevent bank crises due to over-issues of notes. These restrictions encouraged the development of the *cheque system,* and lending by overdraft, though this was not foreseen at the time.

(b) In 1928 the transfer of the Treasury issue to the Bank of England brought about a very large increase in the fiduciary issue, but it was not until 1939 that the note issue became almost entirely fiduciary in character.

(c) After 1939 there was a big increase in the fiduciary issue. The greatest increase in peacetime occurred during 1970–75, as the following figures show:

1928: £260m.	1960: £2,250m.
1939: £580m.	1965: £2,850m.
1946: £1,450m.	1970: £3,500m.
1955: £1,800m.	1975: £5,325m.

5. The size of the fiduciary issue.

(a) The size of the note issue depends on the demand for this sort of cash, this in its turn depending mainly on the level

of bank deposits. The huge increase in the fiduciary issue in recent times is, therefore, a *consequence* of the huge increase in bank deposits.

(b) An increase in the fiduciary issue will increase the liabilities of the Issue Department of the Bank of England, so the assets of this department will be increased by the same amount of Government securities.

6. The supply of coin.

(a) The coins in Great Britain are manufactured by the Royal Mint, the Chancellor of the Exchequer being *ex-officio* its Master. The Mint buys metals in the market and manufactures them into coins for the Bank of England or other customers.

(b) British coins are sold to the Bank of England at their face value, and since the metal content is worth much less than this—all British coins now being merely tokens—the Royal Mint makes a considerable profit.

(c) The Bank of England issues coins to the commercial banks whenever they make withdrawals from their balances (bankers' deposits) in this form of cash.

THE CONTROL OF BANK DEPOSITS

7. The role of a central bank. The main function of a central bank is to control the amount of money in a country. Up to a point the commercial banks themselves determine the level of their deposits (*see* II, **13–15**). If they increase their lending, total bank deposits will also increase; if they curtail their lending, their total deposits will fall. Banks must always be prepared to pay cash on demand to those entitled to ask for it, and so for a long time they maintained a cash ratio of 8 per cent, which experience had taught them was sufficient for this purpose.

The fact that the commercial banks keep approximately half their cash reserves at the Bank of England means that any action by the central bank which affects the balances of the commercial banks will affect their lending policy and, therefore, the total of bank deposits.

Until 1971–72 the Bank of England relied solely on its two traditional instruments of monetary policy, developed during the nineteenth century:

(a) Open-market operations.

(b) Bank rate. (Replaced in 1972 by Minimum Lending Rate.)

In recent years other instruments of monetary policy have been developed.

8. Open-market operations. To influence the cash reserves—and, therefore, the deposits — of the commercial banks, the Bank of England will undertake open-market operations. The Bank's broker will go into the market to buy or to sell securities. Consider the consequences of such actions:

(a) A sale of securities by the Bank of England. The securities sold by the Bank of England, being purchased by customers of the commercial banks, will be paid for by cheques drawn on those banks and paid to the Bank of England. If the total value of these securities is £10 million, the clearing of the cheques will involve a transfer of £10 million from the commercial banks to the Bank of England, this being effected by a reduction of the total balances of these banks at the Bank of England by that amount. Since the commercial banks regarded these balances as cash (rightly so, since withdrawals in cash can be made from them at any time) the effect of the payment for the securities is to reduce the cash reserves and, therefore, the cash ratio of these banks below the level regarded at the time as the minimum for safety. Thus, the commercial banks must set about reducing their deposits in order to restore their liquidity ratio. They will do this in the short run by calling in some of their money at call, but as their liquid assets will have fallen below the required 12½ per cent they will then have to reduce their advances to customers—perhaps refusing to renew some loans and becoming less willing to grant new ones. In this way the quantity of money in the country will be reduced.

(b) A purchase of securities by the Bank of England. In this case the payment for the securities will be made by the Bank of England by means of cheques drawn on itself. Most of these cheques will be paid into branches of the commercial banks, their total deposits thus increasing by (say) £10 million. The clearing of the cheques will require the Bank of England to transfer £10 million to the other banks and this will be done by increasing their balances at the central bank by this amount, thereby raising their liquid assets above 12½ per cent.

This then makes it possible for the banks to increase their advances to customers, thereby expanding their deposits until their liquidity ratio is restored. Thus the quantity of money in the country will be increased.

9. Minimum Lending Rate and Base Rate. In 1972 Bank rate was abolished and replaced by Minimum Lending Rate, both being the rate at which the Bank of England re-discounts bills in its capacity of "lender of last resort". Minimum lending rate was intended solely for this purpose whereas Bank rate had the additional function of influencing many other rates of interest, such as the rate at which banks would make advances to customers and the rate paid by them on deposits. Since 1971, however, the commercial banks have used their own *Base rate* as a basis for their interest rates. Competition between banks keeps their base rates in line. In spite, however, of the changes of 1971–72, it is significant that the commercial banks' base rate have tended to follow the Bank of England's minimum lending rate. The Bank of England always used Bank Rate along with open-market operations.

High interest rates make borrowing generally dear to borrowers—the Government, local authorities, businessmen and individuals—just as low rates make borrowing cheap. When rates are high money is said to be dear and when low money is said to be cheap.

10. New instruments of monetary policy. (*See* also Chapter XIV.) Since 1951 a number of other instruments of monetary policy have been employed.

(a)The Treasury directive. Sometimes known as "moral suasion", at first it took the form of a request from the Treasury to the banks to curtail their lending. More recently the Government has made its wishes known through the Bank of England, which passes on the information to the commercial banks and other financial institutions.

(b) Special Deposits. The Bank of England can ask the commercial banks for Special Deposits in order to reduce their cash reserves. This has a similar effect to a sale of securities in the open market by the Bank of England — it reduces their liquidity ratio and so compels them to curtail their lending.

11. The State and the supply of money.

(a) The note issue. The State's interest has been shown by:

(i) Legislation affecting the denominations of banknotes.

(ii) Legislation limiting the size of the note issue (Act of 1844).

(iii) The Act of 1928 making it necessary to have the consent of the Treasury before the size of the fiduciary issue could be changed.

(iv) The Act of 1954 limiting the fiduciary issue to £1,575 million, although the Treasury was empowered to vary this amount.

(b) Bank Deposits. Until 1914 monetary policy was left to the Bank of England. Since 1919, however, the State has taken an increasing interest in this matter:

(i) From 1919 to 1939 there was co-operation between the Treasury the Governor of the Bank of England.

(ii) Since 1945 the acceptance by the State of responsibility for the control of inflation, the maintenance of full employment, and the balance of payments has made it more directly concerned with monetary policy.

CHAPTER V

THE FINANCIAL MARKETS

The existence of a well-developed money market has been for a long time a distinctive feature of the British banking and financial system. The money and discount markets are considered in **1–9** below and the capital and securities markets in **10–14** of this chapter. The fifth financial market—the foreign exchange market—is discussed in Chapters XIII and XIV.

BILLS OF EXCHANGE

1. Types of bill of exchange. There are two main types of bill of exchange:

(a) The trade bill, used to finance a trade transaction as, for example, to purchase stock or raw material.

(b) The bill of exchange, used simply as a *means of borrowing*. The Treasury bill is the best example of this type of bill.

The wording on a trade bill usually takes the form: *Three months after date of pay to me or my order . . . [the sum involved in words] . . . value received.* Bills of exchange can be drawn for longer or shorter periods than three months.

Since a bill of exchange is drawn on the debtor, it is not valid until it has been accepted by him, when it becomes an *acceptance.*

There are both *inland* and *foreign* bills of exchange. Though employed extensively during the nineteenth century, inland bills are little used today. There has too been a decline in the use of foreign bills during the past 50 years (*see* **8**).

2. Advantages of trade bills. The bill of exchange has advantages for all parties that deal with it:

(a) To the debtor it gives a period of credit during which he is given an opportunity (if he is a merchant) to sell the goods he has bought or (if he is a manufacturer) to turn raw material into a finished product:

(b) To the creditor it provides the possibility of fairly prompt payment if the bill can be discounted for a small

charge at the bank, which in effect then becomes the lender of the sum involved;

(c) To the bank it is a useful asset, since:

(i) It is *short-term.*

(ii) It is *self-liquidating*, being drawn to pay for goods that are to be resold later, and therefore often known as "near money."

(iii) It is a *very liquid* asset, since in an emergency it can be re-discounted.

For these reasons bills of exchange are a very acceptable asset to a bank.

3. Development of the Treasury bill.

(a) Since it was first introduced in 1877 the Treasury bill has been increasingly used by the British Government as a means of short-term borrowing.

(b) It came into use because Government revenue tends to be concentrated into the fourth quarter of the financial year, whereas Government expenditure is more evenly distributed throughout the year.

(c) Nowadays, however, much more than is required for this purpose is borrowed by means of Treasury bills, the total amount outstanding at 31st March 1974 being £5,509 million.

The British commercial banks and discount houses are the principal holders of Treasury bills, but some are held by overseas banks as well as by large industrial and commercial companies.

4. Features of Treasury bills. To bankers, Treasury bills possess the following attractive features:

(a) They are now mainly issued for 91 days (occasionally for 63 days).

(b) They are made available by weekly issues.

(c) They are issued in amounts of £5,000, £10,000, £25,000, £50,000 and £100,000, with a minimum allotment of £50,000.

(d) They can be dated from any day to suit the holder in the week following the Friday on which an offer is made.

It is the amount of Treasury bills offered by the Treasury and taken up by the commercial banks that determines the size of the more liquid assets of these banks and, therefore, the amount of their lending and the extent of their creation of deposits.

5. The issue of Treasury bills. The normal procedure by which Treasury bills are issued is as follows:

(a) The amount to be offered is announced the previous Friday, and printed in the *London Gazette*.

(b) Those desirous of taking up Treasury bills tender for them, that is, they bid a price below the maturity value of the bill to cover interest for the period of the bill.

(c) The principal tender is the syndicated bid of the London discount houses. The commercial banks do not tender directly, but instead obtain bills from the discount houses, but usually not until they have run one month.

(d) Bills are allotted in full to those who have tendered at the hightest price (that is, bearing the lowest rate of interest), and the remainder of the issue at a lower price.

Some Treasury bills are issued "on tap" at a fixed price, but generally only to Government departments—mainly to the Issue Department of the Bank of England.

THE MONEY AND DISCOUNT MARKETS

6. The relation between the money and discount markets.

These two markets are so closely interconnected that they are often regarded as a single market, being then together known as the money market:

(a) The money market (in the most precise sense) is the market for short-term loans. The borrowers in this market are the discount houses, and the lenders are the commercial banks, this item in their balance sheets appearing as "money at call or short notice."

(b) The discount market is mainly concerned with business connected with the discounting of bills of exchange, both trade bills and Treasury bills. The discount houses obtain the funds they require for this purpose from the money market.

7. Members of the money and discount markets. The business of these markets is undertaken by the following institutions:

(a) The Bank of England as "lender of last resort" to the discount houses.

(b) The English commercial banks, which, in addition to lending to the discount houses, also undertake some discount and acceptance business on their own account.

(c) The London agents or branches of overseas banks.

(d) The discount houses and bill brokers, the latter acting as agents for others. The main business of these firms is:

(i) To discount bills of exchange brought to them by or on behalf of merchants and others; and

(ii) To tender for Treasury bills.

(iii) To hold short-term Government bonds.

(e) The acceptance houses (sometimes known as merchant bankers), the banking side of which developed in most cases out of their trading activities. They became acquainted with the financial standing and credit-worthiness of businessmen in those parts of the world with which they traded. This made it possible for them to "accept," for a fee, bills drawn on merchants who were not generally known in London. Such bills then became negotiable on the London discount market.

8. The changed character of the discount market. The work of the discount market has been greatly affected by certain developments:

(a) The decline in the use of trade bills. For inland transactions bills of exchange are now rarely used, and new methods of payment have come to be employed in foreign trade — banks drafts, telegraphic transfers of bank deposits, and documentary credits. Although the bill of exchange is used with the documentary credit, it is drawn on the trader's bank and not on the trader himself. As a result, acceptance business has greatly declined.

(b) The increase in the volume of Treasury bills has offset to some extent the decline in trade bills, but these do not require the special services of the discount houses such as making up in "parcels." Nor do Treasury bills require to be accepted.

9. The discount market today. In recent years the London discount market has widened its activities and adapted itself to changing conditions. To its traditional business of discounting trade bills and Treasury bills it added dealings in short-dated Government stocks before expanding into new fields:

(a) Euro-currency deposits. These are funds deposited with banks in countries other than that of origin, the principal one

being the Euro-dollar dating from 1957, but which had a huge expansion during the 1960s. These funds are mainly used by multi-national companies.

(b) Certificates of deposit (C.D.s). Dating back to 1968, these are negotiable instruments based on bank deposits.

(c) Other negotiable deposits. These include Finance House deposits. Inter-company deposits and Local Authority deposits, all of recent origin.

THE CAPITAL MARKET: I

10. Features of the capital market. In contrast to the money market (the market for very short-term loans) the capital market is a market for longer-term loans. Whereas in the money market loans are for very short periods—from one to fourteen days—loans in the capital market may be for periods as short as three months or for a fixed number of years or for an indefinite period or in perpetuity.

All financial markets, however, are linked together through the rate of interest, funds tending to move to those markets where (other things being equal) the rate of interest is highest.

11. Borrowers in the capital market. Demand in the capital market comes from:

(a) Industrial and commercial undertakings. The capital market is the source from which industry obtains:

(i) Its circulating capital, by advances from the commercial banks of from three to six months, though such loans are renewable.

(ii) Long-term loans by the issue of debentures.

(iii) Permanent capital by the issue of shares.

(b) The British Government, which borrows on long-term by the issue of bonds or stocks repayable after a number of years (for example, 5¾ per cent Funding Loan, 1987–91, repayable any time between those two dates convenient to the Government), or after an indefinite period (for example, 3½ per cent War Loan, after 1952, not yet repaid nor likely to be) or in perpetuity (for example, 2½ per cent Consols, which now carry no date for repayment). For small investors the Government issues National Saving Certificates, National Development bonds and Premium bonds, most of these being redeemable at fairly short notice.

(c) The nationalised industries. At certain periods these industries have been allowed to go to the capital market to raise additional capital by the issue of Government guaranteed stocks such as 3 per cent British Transport stock, 1978-88 and 3 per cent British Gas stock, 1990-95. Like private industry, they often obtain working capital from the commercial banks.

(d) Local authorities. The larger local authorities often borrow from the capital market by the issue of long-term stocks, such as $6\frac{3}{4}$ per cent Greater London Council stock, 1990-92, or by mortgage loans for specified periods of one to ten years, or by the issue of short-term bonds, or by "day-to-day" borrowing at a high rate of interest.

(e) Commonwealth Governments sometimes borrow by the issue of stocks to the London capital market, as for example, $7\frac{1}{2}$ per cent Government of New Zealand stock, 1983-86.

(f) Private individuals, may obtain personal loans from one of the commercial banks, or assistance from hire-purchase companies when buying consumers' goods.

THE CAPITAL MARKET: II

12. Lenders in the capital market. Capital is supplied to the capital market by individuals and institutions:

(a) Private individuals can invest their savings in any of the securities to which reference was made in **11** above.

(b) Companies often finance further expansion from undistributed profits ("company savings"), a process often referred to as "ploughing back" profits into the business.

(c) Insurance companies and private pension funds invest in Government stocks, debentures and shares.

(d) Unit investment trusts, which invest mainly in ordinary shares, enable small investors to spread their investments over a wide field.

(e) Commercial banks make advances to businessmen and private individuals, and also invest in Government stocks.

(f) Trustee savings banks invest their deposits in Government stocks.

(g) Hire-purchase finance companies provide most of the funds required to finance hire-purchase transactions. All the large English commercial banks have hire-purchase subsidiaries.

(h) Finance corporations. The Finance Corporation for Industry (F.C.I.) was established in 1945 to provide medium-term capital for industry. As the F.F.I. (Finance for Industry) its scope was considerably widened in 1974.

13. The securities market. The function of the stock exchange is to make possible the transfer of ownership in stocks and shares. It is essentially, therefore, a market for existing stocks and shares, whereas the capital market is the source of new capital.

There is, however, a close link between the two markets, and "placings" are often made on the stock exchange. The existence of the stock exchange gives liquidity to otherwise illiquid stocks and shares. Without this safeguard, fewer people would be willing to supply capital to the capital market.

14. Stock exchange speculation. The presence of speculators on the stock exchange generally makes it possible for an investor to buy or sell stocks or shares at any time at the prevailing market prices. Such speculators perform a service for ordinary investors.

When, however, speculators try to influence market prices to their own advantage, speculation becomes undesirable.

CHAPTER VI

EXPENDITURE AND REVENUE OF THE STATE

STATE EXPENDITURE

1. Public finance and monetary policy. Since the expenditure of the State can influence the level of employment, Government expenditure is not limited to covering the cost of the many services it now provides, but may be deliberately incurred to finance real capital investment in order to stimulate employment.

Capital expenditure too by businesses can have a similar effect, as also can the level of spendable incomes of individuals.

Taxation, therefore, is no longer simply aimed at covering Government expenditure, but can be increased or decreased to suit the needs of the economic situation or for purposes of social policy. In consequence public finance is now related to monetary theory and practice.

2. Government ordinary expenditure. The main items of Government ordinary expenditure are:

(a) Interest on and management of the National Debt.
(b) Defence—Army, Navy, Air Force.
(c) The maintenance of law and order and the administration of justice.
(d) Education.
(e) Health.
(f) Housing.
(g) Farm subsidies.
(h) Social security—pensions, and national insurance.
(i) Commonwealth and foreign affairs.

During the past 50 years there has been a huge increase of expenditure on social and welfare services.

3. Government loans. In addition to expenditure on current account, as shown in the budget, the Government also incurs expenditure by making loans for various purposes, of which the following are the most important:

(a) Loans to nationalised industries.
(b) Loans to other public corporations.
(c) Loans to local authorities.
(d) Loans for the development of new towns.

STATE REVENUE

4. Government ordinary revenue. Government ordinary revenue comes almost entirely from taxation in one form or another:

(a) Inland revenue:

(i) Income tax.
(ii) Corporation tax.
(iii) Capital transfer tax (replacing Estate duty).
(iv) Stamp duties.

(b) Customs and excise:

(i) Alcoholic drink
(ii) Tobacco.
(iii) Oil.
(iv) Value-added tax (VAT). Two rates since 1975 (petrol at higher rate since 1974).
(v) Other customs and excise duties.

(c) Motor vehicle duties.

5. Other revenue. This revenue comprises mainly the repayment of loans:

(a) Made to nationalised industries.
(b) Made to other public corporations.
(c) Made to local authorities.
(d) Made for the development of new towns.

TAXATION

6. Direct taxes. These are taxes on:

(a) Income—income tax, corporation tax.
(b) Wealth—capital transfer tax, wealth tax, capital levy.

Advantages of direct taxation. Direct taxes can be closely related to ability to pay. They can be progressive, that is, increasing the higher the income, as is the case with both British income tax and capital transfer tax. In addition, there is a surcharge on investment income.

Disadvantages of direct taxation.

(a) A steeply progressive income tax may act as a disincentive and so check production since it falls most heavily on marginal income, such as overtime. This effect is particularly marked when the tax is collected under a PAYE system.

(b) Profits taxes are regarded as a check on enterprise, and may make entrepeneurs less willing to bear risk. Taxes on companies may check investment.

7. Indirect taxes. These are taxes on outlay, that is, on goods and services. They may be imposed either:

(a) To raise revenue.

(b) To protect home industry against foreign competition.

Advantages of indirect taxes. They do not act as a disincentive, but indirect taxation should be spread over as wide a range of goods and services as possible, as is the case with VAT.

Disadvantages of indirect taxes.

(a) They are less related to ability to pay. If imposed on necessaries like foodstuffs they may be regressive. Many taxes, however, such as VAT, are *ad valorem,* with the result that more expensive goods are taxed more heavily than cheaper things. Some goods (*e.g.* food, books) may be exempt.

(b) Although they do not act as a disincentive, they may check the demand for some of the things on which they are imposed.

8. Incidence of taxes. The incidence of a tax is on the persons who pay it:

(a) Income tax falls on the person earning the income — it cannot be passed on to someone else.

(b) Taxes on commodities may fall on the buyers or the sellers or be divided between them, according to the elasticity of demand for the commodity. The more elastic the demand the greater will be the proportion of the tax falling on the seller.

9. Taxable capacity. This is very difficult, if not impossible to calculate. It depends on how the State employs the money collected from taxation. The greater the extent it is used for the provision of services for the people as a whole the greater the amount of taxation they can bear.

10. Local rates. The expenditure of local authorities is covered partly by grants from the Exchequer and partly from local rates, based on the rateable value of land and buildings. This method of assessment results in local rates being only very roughly related to differences in the ability to pay. Since 1965 rebates have been allowed on rates paid by people with low incomes.

THE NATIONAL DEBT

11. The debt of the public sector. This can be classified as follows:

(a) The National Debt:

(i) External debt owing to the United States, Canada and Arab countries, together with any temporary borrowing (e.g. from the I.M.F.).

(ii) Internal debt:

1. Floating (unfunded) debt, *e.g.* Treasury bills, Ways and means advances.
2. Funded (marketable) debt, *e.g.* Consols, Savings Bonds, Exchequer Bonds, Treasury Stock, etc. These stocks are bought and sold on the stock exchange.
3. Non-marketable (also unfunded) debt, *e.g.* Savings Certificates, Premium Bonds.

(b) The debt of local authorities:

(i) Marketable stocks.
(ii) Short-term mortgage loans.
(iii) Short-term bonds.

(c) The debt of nationalised industries: Government guaranteed stocks, such as 3 per cent British Transport Stock 1978–88, 3 per cent British Gas Stock 1990–95.

12. Holders of the British internal debt.

(a) Government departments including the Issue Department of the Bank of England.
(b) Commercial banks (investments).
(c) Other institutional investors, *e.g.* merchant bankers,

discount houses, insurance companies, independent pension funds, investment trust companies, unit investment trusts.

(d) Industrial companies (reserves).

(e) Individual investors.

(f) Overseas banks.

13. The burden of the National Debt.

(a) External debt. If large, this is a serious burden since the interest payments affect the balance of payments.

(b) Internal debt. Since this is owed by the community as a whole to members of the community (interest being merely a transfer payment) it makes a country neither richer nor poorer.

If, however, the debt is large it will increase the general burden of taxation and so may tend to check beneficial expenditure by the Government.

Methods of calculating the burden of interest payments:

(i) As a fraction of Government revenue.
(ii) Per head of the population.
(iii) As a fraction of the national income.

Comparison between one period and another must take account of changes in the value of money.

In spite of the huge increase in the National Debt during the past 200 years the burden of the interest payments per head or as a fraction of the national income is no greater today than it was 150 years ago and it is actually less than it was between the two world wars.

14. Management of the National Debt. According to the *Radcliffe Report* (1959) the National Debt has become "an integral part, even an indispensable part" of the monetary system of Great Britain. One reason for this is the huge increase in the National Debt and the fact that large new issues have to be made each year to replace maturing stocks. Its management is now an important part of monetary policy.

Opportunities for debt management:

(a) When existing stocks reach maturity and are due for repayment.

(b) When new stocks are to be issued.

(c) The holding of securities by Government departments.

To influence the prevailing rate of interest, the Government broker intervenes on the stock exchange to buy or to sell securities. Stocks are bought as they near maturity so that most of new issues are taken up by Government departments and then gradually released to the market. Open-market operations of this kind have developed very considerably since 1945.

PROGRESS TEST 1

THE BRITISH MONETARY SYSTEM

1. It would be difficult for a modern state to do without money. Why? (I, **1-4**)
2. What are the qualities of a good medium of exchange? (I, **6**)
3. Explain the meaning of the phrase "Money is what money does." (I, **10-12**)
4. To what extent can the State decide the type of money to be employed within its borders? (I, **13-15**)
5. It has been said that a country might be able to manage without a medium of exchange but not without a unit of account. Explain. (I, **19-26**)
6. Why is branch banking to be preferred to unit banking? (II, **6**)
7. To what extent is it true to say that nowadays money is created by the banking system? (II, **11, 14**)
8. In what ways is the power of a bank to create credit limited? (II, **15**)
9. What are the main changes that have occurred in recent times in the structure of the balance sheets of the English commercial banks? (II, **18, 19**)
10. Why was the *Bank Charter Act* of 1844 passed? What were the consequences of this Act? (III, **3, 4**)
11. List the main stages by which the Bank of England became a central bank. (III, **6, 13**)
12. What information can be obtained from the Bank return of the Bank of England regarding its main functions? (III, **7, 8, 9-11**)
13. What are the main features that distinguish a central bank from a commercial bank? (III, **13**; IV, **7**)
14. Explain the increase that has taken place this century in the fiduciary issue of the Bank of England (IV, **2-4**)
15. Does an increase in the fiduciary issue necessarily mean that inflation is present? (IV, **5**)
16. Explain the technique of "open-market" operations. What is the purpose of this policy? (IV, **8, 9**)
17. What effects may be expected from changes in Bank rate? (IV, **10**)
18. Compare the traditional instruments of monetary policy — Bank rate and "open-market" operations — with the newer instruments — the Treasury directive and Special Deposits. (IV, **8-10**)
19. What influence does the State have today on the supply of money in Great Britain? (IV, **11**)
20. What are the main differences between a Treasury bill and a trade bill? (V, **1-4**)
21. Describe how Treasury bills are issued. (V, **5**)
22. Is it really possible to distinguished between the money market and discount market? (V, **6**)

23. Make a list of the principal members of the London money and discount market and describe the functions each performs. (V, **7**)

24. Show how the London discount market has adapted itself to the changes that have occurred in recent times. What have been the consequences of these changes? (V, **8**)

25. What is the capital market? What are its main functions? (V, **10-13**)

26. What is the relation between the securities market (stock exchange) and the capital market? (V, **13, 14**)

27. "The budget is no longer merely a financial statement; it has become an instrument of economic policy." Explain this statement. (VI, **1, 14**)

28. Consider the relative merits of direct and indirect taxation. (VI, **6, 7**)

29. Explain the following terms: *(a)* incidence of taxation (VI, **8**); *(b)* taxable capacity (VI, **9**)

30. What is meant by saying that the size of the National Debt is of little importance? (VI, **13**)

PART TWO:

INTERNATIONAL MONETARY RELATIONS

CHAPTER VII

INTERNATIONAL MONETARY TRANSACTIONS

INTERNATIONAL DIVISION OF LABOUR

1. International payments.

(a) Barter persisted much longer for international than it did for internal transactions.

(b) Coins issued by different authorities could be exchanged at a rate based on the relative amounts of precious metal in the various coins.

(c) No international money has yet been devised (though this was considered at Bretton Woods in 1944), but gold has come nearest to serving this purpose.

(d) Currencies that are freely exchangeable for gold are acceptable as means of payment in international dealings. Sterling and the U.S. dollar are used as international currencies today.

2. International trade. Most international payments arise out of trade transactions, that is, they are payments for goods.

(a) At one time countries purchased from others only things which they could not produce for themselves.

(b) The huge expansion of international trade is the result of division of labour being extended to the international sphere—specialisation of production by countries.

3. The Principle of Comparative Cost.

(a) This principle is the basis of the theory of international trade. According to it, total production for the world as a whole will be maximised only if each country specialises in the production of those things for which it has the greatest comparative advantage over others. The goods so produced must then be distributed among the countries demanding them.

(b) Thus, there must be multi-lateral trade, since bi-lateral trade agreements reduce the total volume of trade. This requires there to be no restrictions on trade.

RESTRICTIONS ON FREEDOM OF TRADE

4. Barriers to international specialisation. Some of the obstacles to the free working of the principle of comparative cost are:

(a) Taxes on imports (especially if imposed to protect home industry), imposed either as a permanent tariff or as a temporary "surcharge."

(b) Bounties on exports or tax concessions to encourage exports.

(c) Preferential transport charges on the carriage of goods to ports for export.

(d) Import quotas to restrict imports to specified quantities.

(e) Exchange control—limiting the amount of foreign currency available to the importers of specified goods.

(f) Exchange rates between currencies which do not fairly represent their relative purchasing power.

(g) Insufficient mobility of factors of production, especially of labour.

5. Reasons for action contrary to the Principle of Comparative Cost.

(a) To protect home industry against foreign competition. This makes prices higher in the producing countries and encourages the production of goods in areas where costs of production are high. It is open to less criticism when the aim is to encourage the development of new "infant" industries, but countries are reluctant to remove duties once they have been imposed.

(b) To make a country self-sufficient, that is, not having to depend on others for the things it requires, especially in time of war. There is, however, no economic basis for this policy.

(c) To restore an adverse balance of payments. As a short-term measure, import duties may be imposed or increased or a surcharge imposed on certain classes of imports (as in October 1964) in order to reduce imports. This policy will fail,

however, if other countries retaliate with similar measures. In the long run a restriction of imports will result in a falling off in exports.

6. Regional free trade. Efforts in the past to secure greater freedom of trade had little success. Under GATT (the General Agreement on Tariffs and Trade), set up in 1947, some reductions in tariffs have been agreed, the greatest being those of the Kennedy Round (1964-67). More successful were the two European regional areas of free trade, established in 1957-59:

(a) EEC—The European Economic Community, better known in Britain as the European Common Market, originally comprising Belgium, France, Germany, Italy, Luxembourg and the Netherlands.

(b) EFTA—The European Free Trade Area, at first comprising the United Kingdom, Austria, Denmark, Norway, Portugal, Sweden and Switzerland but later joined by Finland and Iceland.

In 1972 the United Kingdom and Denmark left EFTA and with the Republic of Ireland became members of the EEC. After some modification of the terms, the U.K.'s membership was confirmed in 1975 by a referendum.

THE BALANCE OF PAYMENTS: I—THE "VISIBLE" BALANCE

7. Definition. A balance of payments shows the relationship between all payments made by a country to the rest of the world and its total receipts from all other countries.

8. Composition of the balance of payments. Payments from one nation to another fall into three categories:

(a) Payments arising out of the import or export of goods (*see* **9** below)

(b) Payments for services (*see* **13-15** below)

(c) Capital transfers.

Taken together the balance of payments and receipts under *(a)* and *(b)* provides the balance of payments on current account. If items under *(c)* are included this gives the balance of payments overall.

9. The balance of trade. This is the relationship between payments for imports of goods and receipts from exports of goods. It is also known as the "visible" balance, trade items being regarded as "visible" items. A glance at the table on p.47 shows that the value of Great Britain's imports in 1973 was £13,810 million and that the value of its exports in that year was £11,435 million. This gave a debit balance of £2,375 million, of which oil accounted for £944 million. Except for the years 1956, 1958 and 1971, Great Britain has had an adverse balance of trade for a hundred years. This adverse balance is generally covered by a credit balance in "invisible" items (*see* **13, 14** below)

10. British trade.

(a) Imports into Great Britain comprise mainly:

(i) Foodstuffs.

(ii) Raw materials.

(iii) Some manufactured goods, the quantity of which has tended to increase in recent years. Any expansion of free trade areas or general reduction of tariffs under GATT will probably result in greater specialisation and the import of more manufactured goods by Great Britain.

(b) Exports from Great Britain consist almost entirely of manufactured goods—motor cars, textiles, whisky, etc., together with some partly finished goods. Some imported foodstuffs and raw materials are re-exported (entrepôt trade).

11. Terms of trade. An important influence on the balance of trade is the *terms of trade*, that is, the relation between the general level of prices for imported goods and the prices of exported goods. If export prices are rising more than import prices the terms of trade become "more favourable," and if import prices are arising more than export prices the terms of trade become "less favourable."

When the terms of trade are more favourable it means that a smaller quantity of exports will pay for a given quantity of imports.

12. The British balance of payments. The following table shows the British balance of payments on current account in three recent years:

The British balance of payments

(on current account)

	1967	1970	1973
	£ million	£ million	£ million
Payments (debits)			
1. Imports (visible items): Foodstuffs, Tobacco and drink, Raw materials, Oil	5,674	7,882	13,810 (oil 3,446)
Machinery, etc.			
2. Invisible items: Shipping and air transport, Income from investment, Government expenditure, Travel	2,894	3,912	6,804
Total payments	8,568	11,794	20,614
Receipts (credits)			
1. Exports and re-exports (visible items)	5,122	7,885	11,435
2. Invisible items: Shipping, Income from investment, Travel	3,134	4,540	7,969
Total receipts	8,256	12,425	19,404
Current Balance	—312	+631	—1,210

THE BALANCE OF PAYMENTS: II — THE "INVISIBLE" BALANCE

13. The principal "invisible" items. The most important "invisible" items (*see* page 48) in the British balance of payments are:

(a) Shipping and civil aviation. For a long time Great Britain had a substantial credit balance in the payment for shipping services. In 1950 there was a credit balance of £140 million. More recently, however, income from shipping has been a debit item, although since 1966 this has been generally offset by a credit balance on civil aviation.

(b) Income from foreign investment. During the nineteenth century British investment helped the economic development of countries in many parts of the world. The income from this foreign investment became a very important "invisible" item in the British balance of payments. In spite of many foreign investments having to be sold during the Second World War, British investment abroad has again been built up. Nowadays this is offset to some extent by foreign investment in Great Britain.

(c) Financial services. British banks, insurance companies and other financial institutions derive a considerable income from their foreign business.

14. Other "invisible" items. These include:

(a) Government expenditure abroad. Since 1945 this has been a very large adverse item in the British balance of payments, offset only to a very small extent by the expenditure of the U.S. Government in Great Britain.

The British balance of payments since 1958
(on current account)

\+ = credit balance — = debit balance

	Visible balance	*Invisible balance*	*Net balance*
	£ million	£ million	£ million
1958	+32	+298	+330
1959	−117	+260	+143
1960	−406	+141	−263
1961	−152	+148	−4
1962	−102	+214	+112
1963	−80	+194	+114
1964	−519	+124	−395
1965	−237	+160	−77
1966	−73	+116	+43
1967	−552	+240	−312
1968	−643	+324	−319
1969	−141	+557	+416
1970	+3	+628	+631
1971	+285	+808	+1,093
1972	−677	+791	+114
1973	−2,375	+1,165	−1,210
1974	−5,259 (oil—2,466)	+1,431	−3,828

(b) Travel. This covers the expenditure, whether as tourists or while engaged on business, of British people abroad in relation to expenditure by foreign visitors to Great Britain. It is an almost self-balancing item.

(c) Migrants' funds. Immigrants and foreign workers often send part of their earnings to relatives at home. Emigrants may be allowed to take their savings with them.

15. The balance of payments in recent years. The table on page 48 shows how the British balance of payments has varied from year to year in recent times. During the fifteen years from 1958 to 1972 there were credit balances in nine years and debit balances in only six years, but in 1973 and 1974 there were exceptionally large deficits. These were partly the result of an attempt to stimulate economic growth and partly due to the huge increase in the price of oil.

THE BALANCE ON CAPITAL ACCOUNT

16. Capital transfers. The balance of payments of a country can also be affected by transfers of capital:

(a) For long-term investment abroad.
(b) Short-term, speculative capital movements.

17. Investment abroad. Income from foreign investment, as has already been seen (**13***(b)* above) is a very valuable invisible receipt to the balance of payments on current account. To build up such income it is necessary for investment abroad to have taken place, and when this occurs it is equivalent to a payment abroad. Consequently, investment abroad should occur when a country has a credit or favourable balance of payments on current account.

Capital transfers take place when:

(a) One Government makes a loan to another.
(b) Shares in a foreign company are purchased.
(c) A company establishes a branch abroad.

18. Speculative capital movements. Short-term capital movements, whether into or out of a country, may be quickly reversed, and so can cause instability. Since they are mainly speculative in origin, movement is towards centres of economic strength and away from centres of economic weakness. Consequently, these movements tend to exaggerate the character of a country's balance of payments on current account, strengthening the position when there is a credit balance and increasing a country's difficulties when a deficit is feared.

Most countries, therefore, impose restrictions on investment abroad by their people, whether it is a long-term investment in foreign stocks or shares or in property. Speculative capital movements, however, have proved difficult to control, particularly for a country like Great Britain, since sterling is an international currency held by many foreign banks and other financial institutions.

The following table shows how capital movements have affected the British balance of payments in recent years:

Year	*Balance on current account*	*Capital movements*	*Overall balance*
	£ million	£ million	£ million
1966	+43	=87	=44
1968	=319	=136	=1,077
1970	+631	+499	+1,130
1972	+114	=676	=562
1974	=3,823	+1,147	=2,681

THE QUESTION OF BALANCE

19. International payments must always balance. This is true both of the world as a whole and of each individual country:

(a) The world. Since every export of a country becomes an import to the receiving country, the total for all exports for all countries together must, therefore, be exactly equal. In the same way every payment by one country becomes a receipt to another, so that the total of all international payments must be exactly equal to the total of all international receipts.

(b) Individual countries. Even for a single country an exact balance must be achieved. On current account there may be a favourable (credit) balance or an unfavourable (debit) balance, but over all there must be an exact balance, since the credit or debit balance must be covered in some way.

20. Methods of achieving a balance.

(a) At the present time a debit (alternatively described as *unfavourable, adverse* or *passive*) balance in the balance of payments on current account can be covered in one of the following ways (or a combination of them):

(i) By drawing on the country's gold and convertible currency reserves.
(ii) By borrowing from abroad:

1. From some other country or from a group of countries such as the "Group of Ten" (*see* XVI, **18**)

2. From some international institution such as the International Monetary Fund.

(iii) By purchasing goods from abroad on credit, as may be necessary in time of war.

(iv) By selling foreign investments, as Great Britain had to do during the Second World War.

(b) In the case of a credit (or *favourable* or *active*) balance on current account:

(i) By receiving payment in gold or some convertible currency.
(ii) By increasing investment abroad.

To prevent a recurrence of imbalance more drastic measures may be required. These are considered in **21** below.

21. Methods of correcting an adverse balance of payments. The policy to be adopted by a country in difficulty with its balance of payments will depend very largely on the system of foreign exchange it is operating (*see* Chapters VIII and IX)

(a) Alternative policies:

(i) Deflation, that is, reducing the volume of purchasing power—the normal policy for a country on the gold standard.

(ii) Disinflation—a milder form of deflation—a policy adopted by Great Britain on several occasions during 1949-69.

(iii) Devaluation, that is, reducing the value of a currency in terms of gold—a policy that should be adopted only when there is a "fundamental disequilibrium" in a country's balance of payments when on the gold standard or the Bretton Woods system, as in 1949 and 1967 in the case of sterling.

(iv) Depreciation of the currency on the foreign exchange market, as occurs when exchange rates are free to fluctuate.

(v) Exchange control, either by restriction of supplies of foreign currency or by Government intervention in the foreign exchange market.

(b) Supplementary policies:

(i) Restriction of imports by import duties.
(ii) A temporary restriction of imports by an import surcharge.
(iii) Restriction of imports by quotas, that is, limiting them to stated quantities.

(iv) Stimulation of exports by bounties.

(v) The indirect stimulation of exports by tax concessions or preferential railway rates to the ports (as in Germany in the nineteenth century).

CHAPTER VIII

THE GOLD STANDARD

FOREIGN EXCHANGE

1. The rate of exchange. Payment in international dealings is complicated by each country having its own national currency. Foreign currency (or bank drafts drawn in foreign currency) are required to pay for imports. The demand for foreign currency is, thus, derived from the demand for foreign goods.

How the rate of exchange between two currencies is determined depends on the foreign exchange system in operation at the time.

2. Characteristics of foreign exchange systems. Exchange rates, too, are associated with the problem of the balance of payments. The rate of exchange itself may be the cause of imbalance, causing a "fundamental disequilibrium" in the balance of payments. Each system has its own advantages and disadvantages. In making a choice three considerations have to be born in mind:

(a) Stability of exchange rates, which is undoubtedly advantageous to foreign trade.

(b) Flexibility of exchange rates, which enables a country to retain control over its internal monetary policy.

(c) Free convertibility of currencies, which is essential for the full development of multi-lateral trade.

3. Types of foreign exchange system. During the past hundred years the following systems of foreign exchange have been operated:

(a) The full gold standard down to 1914.

(b) Freely fluctuating exchange rates, operated by most European countries in 1919–25.

(c) The restored gold standard:

(i) The gold bullion standard, adopted by Great Britain in 1925–31.

(ii) The gold exchange standard, operated by the Scandinavian countries, 1925–31.

(d) Exchange control. This followed the collapse of the gold standard.

(i) Restriction, as in Germany, 1931-39, and Great Britain from 1939.

(ii) State intervention in the foreign exchange market, as by Great Britain, France and the United States, 1932-39.

(e) The system adopted under the *Bretton Woods Agreement* (1944) with the establishment of the International Monetary Fund.

The gold standard is discussed in this chapter; the other types of foreign exchange system are considered in Chapter IX.

FEATURES OF THE GOLD STANDARD

4. Relation of currency to gold. When a country is on the gold standard the unit of its currency is declared by law to be equal to a definite weight of gold of a stated degree of fineness. Consequently, there is a fixed price for gold.

If gold coins are issued these must contain precious metal to their full face value and banknotes must be convertible into gold (coins or bullion). When Great Britain had a gold coinage the coins consisted of gold eleven-twelfths fine.

5. Forms of gold standard.

(a) The full gold standard with gold coins in circulation, as employed by many countries before 1914. Banknotes can be exchanged for gold coins on demand.

(b) The gold bullion standard, when gold coins no longer circulate and banknotes can be exchanged only for gold bullion—in Great Britain during 1925–31 gold bars each weighing 400 oz.

(c) The gold exchange standard, under which a country's currency is convertible into the currency of a country on the gold standard but not directly into gold. The currency reserve is in the form of interest-bearing securities of the "parent" country.

6. The three forms of gold standard compared.

(a) Under the full gold standard gold is required both for coins and as a reserve:

(i) Backing for the note issue.

(ii) To cover a deficit in the balance of payments.

(b) The gold bullion standard economises gold, a gold coinage being expensive to maintain, but a gold reserve is required for international payments.

(c) The gold exchange standard still further economises gold, as the reserve may consist mainly of interest-bearing securities of the "parent" country. Gold is expensive to guard and store. The principal drawback to this form of gold standard is dependence on the "parent" country remaining on the gold standard.

THE GOLD STANDARD AND THE INTERNAL SITUATION

7. The quantity of money. On the gold standard the quantity of money in the country is dependent on the amount of gold held:

(a) Coin and notes. The volume of coins and notes can be increased only if additional gold is acquired, and must be decreased if for some reason gold stocks are reduced.

(b) Bank deposits. The volume of bank deposits on the gold standard is dependent on the quantity of cash (if a cash ratio is maintained) and, therefore, ultimately depends on the amount of gold held. Bank deposits can be expanded only if further gold is acquired and, like cash, they must be reduced if gold stocks decline.

8. Variations in the quantity of money. As seen in **4** above, the quantity of money in a country on the gold standard depends on the amount of gold held, variations in the quantity of money being related to changes in this amount.

The quantity of money for internal use, it is said, should be related to the economic needs of the time. For example, an expanding economy requires an expanding supply of money, and it could be argued that at such a time it would be an economically unsound policy to have to reduce the quantity of money on account of an outflow of gold.

With heavy unemployment, as in 1931, it was a serious drawback to the gold standard that an outflow of gold at that time required a reduction in the quantity of money, a policy which checked demand still further and therefore increased unemployment.

9. Prices on the gold standard. Since on the gold standard the price of gold is fixed, changes in demand for or supply of gold cannot influence its price in terms of money but only in terms of what money will buy. An increase in the supply of gold (resulting from increased output from the mines or the discovery of new sources of supply), *other things being equal,* will cause a general rise in the prices of all commodities except gold.

THE GOLD STANDARD AND THE EXTERNAL SITUATION

10. The rate of exchange. The rate of exchange between currencies of countries on the gold standard depends on the relative amount of gold each each is worth. Before 1914 the weight of gold in a sovereign was approximately equal to the amount of gold in a Swiss or French 25 franc piece. The rate of exchange between these currencies was, therefore, approximately £1 sterling = 25 Swiss francs = 25 French francs. This was the *mint par of exchange.* The rate of exchange between two currencies on the gold standard could vary from the mint par of exchange only by the cost of transporting gold in either direction between the two countries. The extreme points of variation in the rate of exchange were, therefore, known as the *specie points.*

11. Gold flows. When a country on the gold standard is running a deficit in its balance of payments, an outflow of gold will occur. In the case of a credit balance there will be an inflow of gold. Thus, on the gold standard, a gold reserve is required for both internal and external use.

An outflow of gold because of a deficit in the balance of payments will *ipso facto* reduce the amount of gold as the basis for the internal money supply. An inflow of gold will have exactly the reverse effect. In either case the effect will be felt first on the quantity of cash. Since the volume of bank deposits is related to the quantity of cash, the monetary authorities (the Bank of England in Great Britain at that time) had to take measures to reduce or increase bank deposits.

12. The "rules" of the gold standard. Thus, a country on the gold standard had to adhere to the following rules:

(a) To deflate when there was an outflow of gold.
(b) To inflate in the case of an inflow of gold.

Deflation required a rise in Bank rate coupled with appropriate "open-market" operations (a sale of securities by the central bank).

Inflation required a reduction in Bank rate and a purchase of securities by the central bank. (*Note.* Inflation in these circumstances would not be very great and would be strictly controlled by the inflow of gold.)

THE "AUTOMATIC" WORKING OF THE GOLD STANDARD

13. The balance of payments on the gold standard. It is said that the gold standard worked automatically, that is, that the effect of an outflow or inflow of gold was to set in motion the very forces which would check the movement and restore equilibrium.

(a) Effect of a debit balance of payments. An outflow of gold, the result of a deficit in the balance of payments, reduces the gold reserves and the cash basis on which bank deposits have been created. The first "rule" of the gold standard has to be obeyed and, therefore, a deflationary policy adopted to reduce the total quantity of money. The effect of this will be to reduce internal prices, including wages (in the days of the full gold standard wages were more flexible than they are today). Imports will remain at their former prices and so the demand for them will fall. The fall in wages will reduce costs of production and so reduce still further the prices of home-produced goods to foreign importers, and this will stimulate foreign demand for them, with the result that exports will expand. The fall in imports and the expansion of exports will eventually wipe out the deficit in the balance of payments.

(b) Effect of a credit balance of payments. A credit balance in the balance of payments will set in motion exactly the reverse series of events, an inflow of gold through inflation leading to a rise in internal prices and wages, an increase in imports and a fall in exports, but again finally resulting in equilibrium.

14. A balance always achieved. The following diagram illustrates the "automatic" working of the gold standard:

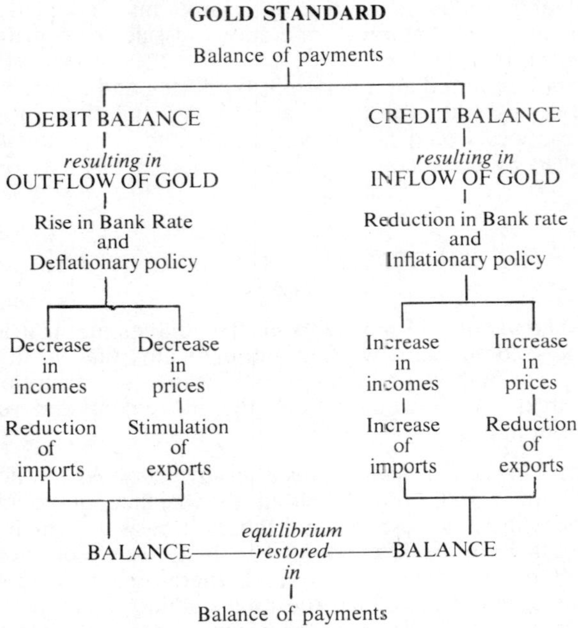

15. Was the gold standard self-regulating? The account of the "automatic" working of the gold standard described in **13** and **14** above is that given in the report of the *Cunliffe Committee*, which had been set up in 1918 to consider whether it was desirable to restore the gold standard. It recommended this course and in 1925 Great Britain returned to the gold standard.

16. Some criticisms of the Cunliffe report.

(a) Though the gold standard worked very well before 1914 the *Cunliffe Committee's* explanation is very much over-simplified.

(b) In any case, the gold standard worked automatically only if central banks adhered strictly to the "rules."

(c) Any action taken by a central bank would be slow to take effect.

(d) It depends too much on the Quantity Theory of money (*see* X, **12-16**), and this theory has been severely criticised.

(e) Too much importance is, perhaps, attached to Bank rate changes.

(f) No account is taken of the effect of capital movements.

Experience of the chaotic conditions of foreign exchange and runaway inflation after the First World War made the gold standard appear particularly attractive.

ADVANTAGES AND DISADVANTAGES OF THE GOLD STANDARD

17. Advantages

(a) Stability of exchange rates, which is advantageous to international trade.

(b) Provided the "rules" were followed there was no danger of run-away inflation, although in an emergency a currency might be devalued.

(c) The balance of payments could be left to take care of itself.

18. Disadvantages

(a) The total supply of money is too rigidly related to a country's supply of gold.

(b) Through the gold reserve, it links a country's internal monetary policy too rigidly to the requirements of the external situation.

(c) An independent monetary policy suited to the needs of the internal situation cannot be followed.

THE COLLAPSE OF THE GOLD STANDARD

19. General causes.

(a) Many countries did not keep to the "rules":

(i) Countries receiving gold were often unwilling to inflate, as they feared a rise in prices would harm their export trade, and so the gold they received was "sterilised."

(ii) Those losing gold were often unwilling to deflate, especially if they were already suffering from heavy unemployment, which they feared would be made worse by deflation.

(b) Wages and other costs of production tended to be more "sticky" than in pre-1914 days and so deflation was more likely to lead to a rise in unemployment than to a fall in prices.

(c) Speculative capital movements, arising from the growth of a mass of short-term funds, the owners of which were more concerned for the safety of their capital than the return on it. Immediately there was a hint of crisis in a centre, these funds would be withdrawn, thereby exaggerating the difficulties of the country from which they had been moved.

(d) Somewhat similar to *(c)* were the actions of countries on the gold exchange standard which, to protect their reserves, would withdraw funds from the "parent" country at the mere hint of danger.

(e) Maldistribution of gold, largely as a result of the war, among the countries on the gold standard — the United States having too much while many countries had too little.

(f) Interest payments on inter-Allied war debts.

(g) The payment of reparations by countries defeated in the war.

Causes *(e)*, *(f)* and *(g)* were all direct consequences of the war; *(c)* was the result of the chaotic monetary conditions immediately after the war and so it too was an indirect consequence of the war.

20. Causes particularly affecting Great Britain. The general causes listed in **19** above all affected Great Britain. In addition Britain had some other difficulties of its own:

(a) The return to the gold standard in 1925 had been made at the pre-1914 parity with the US dollar of 4.86⅔. This was thought to be necessary if Great Britain was to retain its pre-1914 financial prestige, from which considerable "invisible" income was derived. Great Britain was, however, economically weaker in 1925, whereas the United States, having been an active belligerent for less than a year, had increased enormously in economic strength.

(b) Great Britain had suffered very heavy shipping losses during the war and other countries had been able to build up their mercantile marines, so that Britain could no longer retain the overwhelming share of the carrying trade of the world that it had had during the nineteenth century.

21. Immediate causes of Great Britain leaving the gold standard. The sequence of events was as follows:

(a) Both Great Britain and the United States had made long-term loans to Germany to help that country's economic development in order to enable it to pay reparations.

(b) Large amounts of three-months British Treasury bills were held by foreign institutions.

(c) Great Britain was thus said to be "lending long and borrowing short."

(d) In 1929 came the Wall Street crash in New York and the cessation of US lending to Germany.

(e) Germany declared a moratorium. As a result, Great Britain could not secure repayment of debts, whereas funds could be withdrawn from Britain.

(f) The British budget of April 1931 showed a large deficit.

(g) Fearing that Great Britain would be unable to stay on the gold standard, both speculators and the central banks of countries on the gold exchange standard began to withdraw funds from London.

(h) There was a heavy outflow of gold from Great Britain in spite of loans from the United States and France.

(i) In September 1931 Great Britain left the gold standard. Although the country had credit balances in its balances of payment on current account in 1929 and 1930 and a debit balance in 1931 of only £104 million, it suffered over the three years a "flight of capital" of £270 million, giving it an increasing overall debit balance for these three years.

CHAPTER IX

ALTERNATIVES TO THE GOLD STANDARD

FLEXIBLE OR "FLOATING" EXCHANGE RATES

1. The rate of exchange.

(a) On the gold standard the rate of exchange between different currencies, it will be remembered, depended on:

(i) The amount of gold in the coins (or the amount of gold the standard unit of a currency was declared to be worth).

(ii) The convertibility of notes for gold in large or small quantities.

(b) Off the gold standard, with rates of exchange free to fluctuate (or "float"), the rate of exchange becomes the price of one currency in terms of another, determined like other prices, in the market (in this case, the foreign exchange market) by the interplay of the forces of supply and demand.

2. The demand for and supply of foreign currency.

(a) Demand for a currency is determined by a country's demand for imports.

(b) Supply of a currency depends on a country's exports.

Thus, the rate of exchange depends on the relation between a country's imports and its exports.

(i) Depreciation of a currency. An increased demand for imports will increase the price of foreign currency, so that the rate of exchange for the home country's currency will fall, that is, it will depreciate. A fall in its exports will have a similar effect.

(ii) Appreciation of a currency. A fall in the demand for imports will reduce the price of foreign currency, so that the rate of exchange for the home currency will rise, that is, it will appreciate. A rise in exports will have a similar effect.

3. World-wide rates of exchange. With flexible exchange rates in general operation the rate of exchange between each pair of currencies will be determined in this way. Any discrepancies that might arise between the rates in foreign exchange markets in different centres will be ironed out as a result of *arbitrage* — the purchase of currency in centres where it is cheap and its transfer to centres where it can be sold at a profit.

The result is a world-wide market in foreign exchange with a single set of prices.

4. The balance of payments.

(a) Thus with flexible exchange rates any change in a country's imports or exports immediately affects the rate of exchange for its currency.

(b) This keeps its balance of payments in equilibrium. An adverse balance of payments causes its currency to depreciate, thereby:

(i) Checking imports by making foreign goods dearer.
(ii) Encouraging exports, which become cheaper to foreign buyers.

A favourable balance of payments would have exactly the opposite effect.

(c) Thus, with flexible exchange rates, as on the gold standard, any disequilibrium in the balance of payments will itself set in motion the forces which will would restore equilibrium.

FEATURES OF FLEXIBLE EXCHANGE RATES

5. Advantages.

(a) A country, so it said, can adopt whatever internal monetary policy it pleases. It certainly never need adopt a deflationary policy which is bound to be unpopular (but *see* **6** *(b)* below).

(b) It is relieved of concern for its gold reserves, since its currency is not convertible into gold.

(c) The balance of payments can be left to take care of itself.

6. Disadvantages.

(a) A rate of exchange which can vary from day to day adds to the uncertainty of foreign trade, although this can be reduced to some extent by the development of a forward exchange market.

(b) There is no effective check on inflation as on the gold standard. This places greater responsibility, therefore, on the monetary authorities than does the gold standard. A government, never needing to deflate, may shirk the unpopular policies necessary to balance its budget. The result

will then be a continuous depreciation of the currency and the danger of a runaway inflation.

Although in theory a country operating this system can pursue an independent internal monetary policy it cannot ignore its effect on the external value of its currency.

Flexible exchange rates, operated by many countries after the First World War, became discredited on account of the serious inflations that occurred during that period. Sterling, however, was again allowed to "float" in 1972 (*see* p.123).

THE "PURCHASING POWER PARITY" THEORY

7. Outline of the theory. This theory was put forward to explain the determination of the rate of exchange when a system of flexible exchange rates is in operation and currencies are not linked to gold.

According to this theory the rate of exchange between two currencies depends on their relative purchasing power in their home countries, allowance being made for cost of transport and any indirect taxes levied on them.

Thus, if a certain assortment of goods costs 20 DM in Germany and the same assortment of goods costs 2,000 *lire* in Italy, the rate of exchange between these two currencies should be 1 DM= 100 *lire*.

8. Criticisms of the theory.

(a) It is true that the internal value of a currency influences its external value. A steep rise in internal prices will certainly cause a currency to depreciate on the foreign exchange market, but not every slight change in internal purchasing power will affect the rate of exchange. The theory implies a closer connection between the internal purchasing power of different currencies than actually exists.

(b) In any case, it is extremely difficult to compare the value of money in different countries, since different peoples do not buy the same assortments of goods. The price of spaghetti or wine is of more importance to an Italian than to a British housewife, but with beef and tea the reverse applies.

(c) Since rates of exchange depend on the demand for the currencies and their supply in the foreign exchange market, and the demand and supply of currency are determined by the demand for imports and exports, only the prices of goods

that enter into international trade and not those produced solely or mainly for home consumption influence rates of exchange. An increase in demand for an imported commodity will cause the importing country's currency to depreciate and, therefore, make *all* its imports dearer and *all* its exports cheaper, while the prices of home-produced goods remain unchanged.

(d) Capital movements influence the rate of exchange without any change in the relative purchasing power of currencies. Speculative capital movements are likely to be more frequent on a system of flexible exchange rates than on the gold standard.

(e) Non-monetary influences can affect the rates of exchange, especially political changes and anticipated effects of Government policy — taxation changes, a new parliamentary bill, Cabinet changes, a general election, a foreign crisis, etc.

EXCHANGE CONTROL

9. Dislike of flexible exchange rates. When the revived gold standard collapsed in the early 1930s few countries wanted to return to the system of flexible exchange rates that had prevailed during the years following the First World War:

(a) To Germany and some others that system was associated with runaway inflation.

(b) Others had suffered varying degrees of inflation.

(c) All countries felt that violently fluctuating exchange rates were bad for international trade, and speculative capital movements tended to exaggerate such fluctuations.

The result was that some countries introduced exchange control immediately on leaving gold, while others went over to free exchange rates for time to allow their currencies "to find their true level," afterwards introducing some form of exchange control.

10. Aims of exchange control. A country may impose exchange control for one of the following reasons:

(a) To keep the exchange rate of its currency stable, that is, to give it the main advantage of the gold standard without the drawbacks.

(b) To avoid the possibility of a runaway inflation. This had occurred so recently in Germany that a return to free exchange rates would probably have resulted in an immediate attempt by the German people to protect their new savings by an export of capital or the purchase of property or other durable goods. This would have caused an immediate and catastrophic depreciation of the currency, from the loss of confidence in it.

(c) To insulate the rate of exchange as far as possible from the effects of capital movements, but to permit fluctuations in the rate due to the effect of transactions on current account.

(d) A country may deliberately under-value its currency in order to stimulate its exports (as a result cheaper to foreign buyers) and check imports (dearer now to its own people). If other countries retaliate it is likely to lead to competitive devaluation of currencies.

(e) A country may deliberately over-value its currency for reasons of prestige (as Great Britain did in 1925 on its return to the gold standard). It would also be of some advantage to a country with a heavy foreign debt. It could not be maintained for long, however, unless there was a fairly inelastic demand for the country's exports. Thus, during 1945–49 sterling could have been over-valued to a greater extent than it was, but devaluation in 1949 would then have had to be even more drastic. In 1945–49 valuation of sterling was advantageous to Great Britain but disastrous in 1925–31.

METHODS OF EXCHANGE CONTROL

11. Restriction. Under this system of exchange control, the amount of foreign currency people are allowed to acquire is restricted. This is particularly necessary if the currency is over-valued, since in such circumstances demand is likely to exceed supply.

12. Features of restriction—Germany, 1931–39.

(a) All applications for foreign currency have to be submitted to the central bank, which can then decide the purposes for which it can be used. When Germany imposed restriction in 1931 it was used to regulate its import trade, so that after 1934 imports came to be limited to materials

required for re-armament. Applications for foreign currency for private purposes were almost always refused.

(b) Foreign holdings of German currency were placed in blocked accounts. This reduced trade with Germany.

(c) Multiple exchange rates were introduced, with different rates according to the purpose for which the currency was required.

(d) Foreign tourists were offered an advantageous rate of exchange, as Germany soon began to find it difficult to acquire foreign exchange, the effect of *(b)* having been to make foreigners reluctant to trade with Germany.

13. Effects of restriction, 1931-39. For a time, foreign trade with Germany almost came to a standstill. In order to protect exporters who sold goods to Germany from the risk of payment being blocked, foreign governments entered into clearing or payments agreements with Germany. Trade was almost reduced to barter.

14. Great Britain and restriction. Great Britain did not introduce restriction until the outbreak of war in 1939. The sterling-dollar rate was fixed and payment for imports was placed in blocked accounts, as Great Britain could only buy on credit during the war and little was produced for export. After the war, restriction was retained and applications for foreign currency had to be made to the Bank of England. The personal allowance for foreign travel was gradually increased, and during 1959–66 restriction has applied only to the export of capital From 1966 to 1969 there were restrictions on foreign travel.

INTERVENTION

15. Intervention in the market. In this case the Government does no more than intervene in the foreign exchange market, either to buy or sell foreign currency or its own. After leaving the gold standard in 1931 Great Britain for a time went over to freely fluctuating exchange rates to allow sterling "to find its own level." In March 1932 intervention in the market began. The aim of British intervention was:

(a) At first, to reduce the effect on the rate of exchange for sterling of speculative capital movements.

(b) Later, to maintain a fairly stable rate of exchange.

16. The British Exchange Equalisation Account. A department of the Treasury set up by the British Government in 1932 to be responsible for official intervention in the foreign exchange market, its policy was to offer foreign currency to the market if others were selling sterling and to see sterling if there was a greater demand for it than the available supply. To carry out such a policy, sufficient supplies of foreign currency are required to match sales of sterling.

After 1932, however, the demand for sterling was increasing and so the British Exchange Equalisation Account was able to build up supplies of foreign currency.

The Account operated in gold standard currencies — at first in dollars and later in French francs. The Account nowadays turns the convertible currencies it acquires into gold and obtains its sterling by the issue to it of Treasury bills.

The British Account intervened in the foreign exchange market during 1949–67 to keep the sterling-dollar ratio within the range 2.78 and 2.82 and again during 1967–72 within the limits of 2.38 and 2.42 US dollars to the pound sterling. Since 1972 the Exchange Equalisation Account has intervened occasionally to influence the sterling exchange rate.

Exchange equalisation accounts also provided a means by which countries could "sterlise" inflows of gold—that is, prevent its influencing the internal monetary supply.

17. A regional gold standard.

(a) Other countries followed Great Britain's example in setting up an exchange equalisation account (known in the United States as the Exchange Stabilisation Fund).

(b) In 1936 Great Britain, France and the United States made the *Tripartite Agreement*, under which each country undertook to buy from the others for gold any of its own currency they acquired. The rates of exchange between the three currencies were generally regarded as fixed but were subject to adjustment by agreement with the other two parties if a serious disequilibrium occurred.

(c) This was equivalent to a return to a modified—and less rigid—form of gold standard on a regional basis. A number of other countries joined the scheme.

INTERNATIONAL MONETARY CO-OPERATION (1944)

18. The Bretton Woods Conference, 1944.

(a) The conference at Bretton Woods in the United States was called to devise an international monetary system to be operated after the Second World War.

(b) The restrictionist practices of the period before 1939 were condemned—multiple exchange rates, unilateral blocking of accounts, bilateral trading agreements, restrictionist types of exchange control.

(c) The aim was to encourage multi-lateral trade. To achieve this it was necessary for:

(i) All currencies to be freely convertible.

(ii) Exchange rates to be stable.

(iii) Assistance to be given to a country in *temporary* difficulty with its balance of payments.

19. The Bretton Woods scheme. Although the gold standard gave stable exchange rates and free convertibility of currencies, it was regarded as too rigid a system.

The scheme adopted at Bretton Woods was a compromise between the plans put forward by the British and American Treasuries. The two plans were very similar but the British plan, largely the work of Lord Keynes, would have considerably increased international liquidity.

Under the agreed scheme, two international institutions were established — the International Monetary Fund and the International Bank for Reconstruction and Development (better known as the World Bank).

20. The International Monetary Fund (IMF). The chief features of the IMF are:

(a) Members have to assign gold parities to their currencies.

(b) Changes of parity were permissible:

(i) Up to 10 per cent, merely by notifying the Fund.

(ii) Above 10 per cent but less than 20 per cent, with the permission of the Fund, which had to give its decision within 72 hours.

(iii) Above 20 per cent, only after consideration by the Fund, its decision not being restricted by any time limit.

(c) Currencies were to be freely convertible, but this clause was to be waived for a transition period of five years after the ending of the war.

(d) Each member had to contribute to the IMF's pool a certain sum, 25 per cent in gold (or US dollars) and the remainder in its own currency, each member being assigned by the IMF a quota for this purpose.

(e) The lending resources of the IMF were increased in 1964 by the "Group of Ten"—ten countries, including Great Britain, the United States, France and Germany, which agreed to lend to the Fund if required.

(f) A member in difficulties with its balance of payments was entitled to assistance from the Fund, being permitted to purchase foreign currency from the Fund up to a maximum of 25 per cent of its quota in any one year, but if the Fund possessed an amount of a member's currency in excess of double its quota that member could obtain foreign currency only in exchange for gold. Thus, although quotas were increased in 1959, and again in 1965, a country's drawings on the Fund were sufficient only to cover a relatively small deficit in its balance of payments, though a member country in particular difficulty could apply for additional assistance. A member expecting to draw on the Fund could arrange with it a "stand-by agreement," the amount being agreed in advance so that drawings, if required, could be made without delay. Drawings had to be repaid within three to five years.

The headquarters of the International Monetary Fund is in the United States, at Washington, D.C.

21. The International (or World) Bank (IB). Membership of the International Bank for Reconstruction and Development is restricted to countries that are members of the IMF. Its capital has been provided partly by the members on a quota basis and partly by borrowing on the world capital market. With its headquarters also at Washington D.C., the World Bank, like the IMF, was established by the Bretton Woods conference.

Its purpose is to give a greater amount of assistance where required than the IMF can provide, such as loans to cover reconstruction or capital development. Loans for specific development projects are granted principally to governments and only to companies if the loans are government-guaranteed.

In 1956 the World Bank established a subsidiary, known as the International Finance Corporation, to provide assistance for private enterprise in under-developed countries. The work of the IB is also supplemented by the International Development Association (IDA).

PROGRESS TEST 2

INTERNATIONAL MONETARY RELATIONS

1. Why did barter persist for so much longer a period of time in international trade than in internal trade? (VII, **1**)

2. How did gold coins, minted by different issuing authorities serve as means of payment in international trade? (VII, **1**)

3. Account for the huge increase in the volume of international trade during the past hundred years. (VII, **2**)

4. Enunciate the principle on which the theory of international trade is based. (VII, **3**)

5. What are the main hindrances in the actual conditions of international trade to the free working of the principle of comparative cost? (VII, **4**)

6. If all countries of the world permitted the free working of the principle of comparative cost, it is said, the total output of all kinds of goods for the world as a whole would be at its maximum. This being so, how do you account for countries in actual conditions acting contrary to this principle to the extent they do? What form do these hindrances take? (VII, **4, 5**)

7. Describe the main attempts made since 1945 to give more free play to the working of the Principle of Comparative Cost. (VII, **6**)

8. Why do countries often import goods which they themselves are able to produce? Why do they sometimes export goods which their own people would like to have? (VII, **1-5**)

9. Distinguish between *(a)* the balance of trade and the balance of payments, and *(b)* the balance of payments on current account and on capital account. (VII, **7, 8**)

10. How far is it true to say that a country's exports pay for its imports? (VII, **8-10**)

11. What are the main types of goods that enter into British import and export trade? (VII, **10**)

12. What is meant by the terms of trade? Show how changes in the terms of trade may affect a country's balance of payments. (VII, **11**)

13. List the principal "invisible" items in the British balance of payments. Comment on any changes that have taken place during the past thirty years in the importance of these items. (VII, **13, 14**)

14. Compare the effects of long-term and short-term capital movements on a country's balance of payments. (VII, **16-18**)

15. What is meant by saying that a country's balance of payments must always balance? (VII, **19, 20**)

16. Explain the meaning of the following terms: *(a)* deflation; *(b)* disinflation; *(c)* devaluation; *(d)* depreciation. (VII, **21**)

17. Distinguish between *(a)* the full gold standard; *(b)* the gold bullion standard; *(c)* the gold exchange standard. (VIII, **3, 5, 6**)

18. Show how inflows and outflows of gold affect the internal supply of money on the gold standard. (VIII, **7, 8**)

19. How is the rate of exchange determined between the currencies of two countries, both on the gold standard? (VIII, **10**)

20. What were the so-called "rules" of the gold standard? (VIII, **12**)

21. What is meant by saying that the gold standard worked "automatically"? How far was this true? (VIII, **13-15**)

22. Why was the gold standard-restored in the 1920s? What brought about the collapse of the gold standard in the 1930s? Why did Great Britain find it difficult to stay on the gold standard? (VIII, **19-21**)

23. How is the exchange rate between two currencies determined when the countries concerned are both operating a system of free exchange rates? (IX, **1, 2**)

24. What is meant by saying that the market in foreign exchange is a world-wide market? What makes it so? (IX, **3**)

25. On a system of freely fluctuating exchange rates the balance of payments, it is said, is automatically brought into balance. Explain this statement. (IX, **4**)

26. Every system of foreign exchange has both advantages and disadvantages. Is this true? (VIII, **17, 18**; IX, **19, 20**)

27. Critically examine the Purchasing Power Parity theory of foreign exchange. (IX, **7, 8**)

28. For what purposes may a country adopt exchange control? Why did Germany introduce so far-reaching a system of exchange control in 1931? (IX, **9, 10**)

29. Distinguish between "restriction" and "intervention" as methods of exchange control. (IX, **11-14**)

30. What were the functions of the British Exchange Equalisation Account in the 1930s? What are its functions at the present day? (IX, **15, 16**)

31. Explain the terms "over-valuation" and "under-valuation" when used of a country's currency. (IX, **18, 19**)

32. Why did the nations of the world think a new system of foreign exchange was required after the Second World War? (IX, **18**)

33. Consider the part played by gold in the Bretton Woods scheme. (IX, **19**)

34. Show how the International Monetary Fund attempted to serve the interests of its members. (IX, **20**)

35. What are the functions of the World Bank? (IX, **21**)

PART THREE:

MONEY AS A DYNAMIC FACTOR

CHAPTER X

THE VALUE OF MONEY

MONEY, VALUE AND PRICE

1. Value is subjective.

(a) The value of a thing depends on the amount of satisfaction to be derived from it. Since value is subjective, people do not attach the same value to a commodity at a particular time, nor does the same person attach the same value to a thing at different times. This is also true of money, for the poor man would attach more value to an addition of 50p to his income than would a rich man.

(b) Economic theory shows too that value cannot be measured.

2. Money as a measure of value. If value is subjective, money cannot serve efficiently as a measure of value (I, **19-26**). Nevertheless, it is undoubtedly very convenient for purposes of trade to attach prices to goods in terms of money, and this is a particularly useful function of money.

3. Value and price.

(a) The fact that one article is three times the price of another does not, therefore, mean that it has three times the value of the other. Value and price are clearly not the same thing. However, when making a purchase a person has to decide whether he regards the price as a fair assessment of the value of the commodity to him.

(b) The value of money can be seen only through the prices of other goods. The value of money is what money will buy. The general price level is taken as the indicator of the value of money, though strictly its value can be considered only in relation to single articles.

(c) Used in connection with price, money becomes a unit of measurement, but unlike other units of measurement—metres and kilometres, grams and kilograms, tons and hundredweights—it is itself liable to variation.

4. The price of money. Confusion occurs as a result of regarding value and price as synonymous. A further difficulty arises because different meanings are attached to the terms *value of money* and *price of money:*

(a) The value of money = what money will buy.

(b) The price of money = the price paid for the use of money, that is, the rate of interest.

CHANGES IN THE VALUE OF MONEY

5. The three trends. Three distinct trends have been noticed in variations in the value of money:

(a) The long-period tendency for the value of money to fall, that is, for prices to rise.

(b) The medium-term fluctuations of the nineteenth century associated with the relation between the world output of gold and industrial productivity.

(c) The short-term fluctuations associated with the trade cycle.

6. The long-period trend. Although during the past thousand years there have been periods when the value of money has been rising, such periods have usually been of relatively short duration. The value of money has generally been less at the end of a century than it was at the beginning. This has certainly been the case in recent centuries, though the price fluctuations of particular commodities have sometimes been contrary to the general trend.

Thus, although most things were dearer in 1900 than in 1801, books were cheaper. In past centuries the fall in the value of money was often—though not always—very gradual, but the two great wars of the twentieth century and their aftermath caused an exceptionally severe fall in the value of money during the first half of this century, and present Government policies with regard to full employment and economic growth are likely to be associated with a continuing fall in the value of money despite efforts to check it.

7. Medium-term fluctuations. During the nineteenth century the supply of money was closely related to the supply of gold. During periods when the output of gold was greatly expanded owing to the discovery of new sources of supply, the quantity of money also increased and prices tended to rise; whereas during periods of increased industrial productivity due to technical progress there was a tendency for prices to fall. Thus:

(a) 1820–49 was a period of falling prices.

(b) 1849–74, following discoveries of gold in California, Russia and Australia during 1847–51, was a period of rising prices.

(c) 1874–96 was again a period of increasing productivity; there was also an increased demand for gold as more countries went over to the gold standard, and as a result it was a period of falling prices.

(d) 1896–1914, owing to further discoveries of gold in South Africa during 1884–5, was again a period of rising prices.

8. Short-term price movements. The trade cycle was a pronounced feature of industrial activity throughout the nineteenth century and the early years of the twentieth century. Boom periods succeeded one another at regular intervals of seven or eight years, with a depression between each. Prices tended to rise as depression gave way to boom and then to fall as boom turned into depression.

MEASUREMENT OF CHANGES IN THE VALUE OF MONEY

9. Indexes of prices. Attempts have been made to measure changes in the value of money by means of indexes of prices. The principle adopted in all cases is to select a base year and assign to it the number index 100. The prices for a selected group of commodities are then noted. A decrease in the value of money (that is, a rise in prices) is then shown by a rise in the index number. At first indices were compiled only for wholesale prices.

(a) Indexes of wholesale prices:

(i) The Sauerbeck index (37 commodities).
(ii) The Board of Trade Index (150 commodities).
(iii) The *Economist* index.
(iv) The *Digest of Statistics* index (base year 1954).

Separate indices are calculated for different groups of related commodities.

(b) Index of retail prices. Since 1914 the Department of Employment (then the Ministry of Labour) has compiled an index of retail prices, known until 1947 as the "cost of living index."

10. Difficulties in compiling a retail price index.

(a) The choice of commodities to be included.

(b) The "weighting" to be attached to each commodity. The method adopted is to take a survey of the expenditure of people within a selected income range.

(c) The higher the income the greater is the variation between different individuals' expenditure.

(d) Tastes and fashions change with changes in the general standard of living. Thus, periodic revision of the index is necessary.

(e) Changes in quality may hide changes in prices.

(f) Comparison over long periods of time is not possible.

11. Weighting of the index of retail prices. The following table shows the different weights adopted at various times for the index of retail prices:

Commodity groups	1914	1947	1952	1956	1062	1970
	%	%	%	%	%	%
I. Food	60	34.8	39.9	35.0	31.9	23.2
II. Alcoholic drink	—	21.7	16.8	7.1	6.3	8.2
III. Tobacco	—			8.0	7.7	4.6
IV. Housing	16	8.8	7.2	8.7	10.4	10.9
V. Fuel and light	8	6.5	6.6	5.5	6.3	5.3
VI. Durable household goods	—	7.1	6.2	6.6	6.4	7.0
VII. Clothing and footwear	12	9.7	9.8	10.6	9.8	8.9
VIII. Transport and vehicles	—	—	—	6.8	9.3	14.9
IX. Miscellaneous	4	3.5	4.4	5.9	6.3	7.1
X. Services	—	7.9	9.1	5.8	5.6	5.2
XI. Meals taken outside home	—	—	—	—	—	4.8
	100	100.0	100.0	100.0	100.0	100.0

Since 1962 the weights have been revised annually. In February 1975 the indices for the main groups were as follows (15 January 1974 = 100):

All items 143.0

I. 120.5	VII. 118.3
II. 118.3	VIII. 118.6
III. 118.2	IX. 130.3
IV. 124.0	X. 125.2
V. 110.3	XI. 115.8
VI. 124.9	XII. 118.7

Separate indices are compiled not only for the main groups but also for the sub-divisions within the groups. For example, indices for the sub-divisions of Group I in October 1970 were:

Bread, flour, cakes	128
Meat	107
Fish	103
Butter, margarine, lard	135
Milk, cheese, eggs	93
Tea, coffee, cocoa	129
Sugar, preserves	190
Vegetables	131
Fruit	128

The effects of changes in the value of money are considered in Chapter XI.

THE QUANTITY THEORY OF MONEY

12. The early quantity theory. In the sixteenth century:

(a) Prices were rising more rapidly than in earlier times.

(b) The quantity of money was increasing as a result of increased supplies of silver, the principal monetary metal.

Bodin, therefore, put forward an early, crude form of the quantity theory of money: the value of money varies in direct proportion to changes in the quantity of money.

13. The refined quantity theory. The old quantity theory of money was revived after the First World War and refined by *Irving Fisher* to explain the great inflations of those days.

Refinements introduced by Fisher:

(a) He distinguished between bank deposits and cash.

(b) He introduced the concept of the velocity of circulation, that is, the rate at which money changes hands.

(c) He also showed the influence of the volume of production.

14. The equation of exchange. This summarises the quantity theory in the following equation:

$$MV = PT$$

or

$$MV + M'V' = PT$$

The symbols represent:

M=all kinds of money (in the first equation) or cash only (in the second equation);

M'=bank deposits;

V V'=the velocity of circulation of the type of money to which it is attached;

P=the general price level;

T=the total number of monetary transactions that have taken place during the period concerned.

15. In favour of the Quantity Theory.

(a) It shows that the value of money can be affected by influences other than the quantity of money:

(i) An increase in the velocity of circulation has a similar effect to an increase in the quantity of money.

(ii) An increase in production can offset the effect of an increase in the quantity of money.

(b) There *is* some connection between the quantity of money and the general price level in the long period.

16. Criticisms of the Quantity Theory.

The theory, however, has been subjected to severe criticism:

(a) It shows only how *changes* in the value of money are brought about; it does not explain how the *value* of money is in the first place determined.

(b) It pays too much attention to supply, which is only one of two forces affecting value, though velocity of circulation is not unrelated to demand (*see* **19** below).

(c) The four variables of the quantity equation are not independent of one another, for money itself is a dynamic force in the economy:

(i) A change in M may itself influence V.

(ii) A change in M may also affect T.

The theory implies too precise a relationship between these four variables.

(d) All prices do not always rise or fall together or to the same extent; there are sectional price levels for related groups of commodities rather than a general price level.

(e) It takes no account of the rate of interest.

THE DEMAND AND SUPPLY THEORY OF MONEY

17. The value of money. The value of a commodity is determined by the influence of the two forces of demand and supply on one another. It is suggested, therefore, that the value of money can be explained in the same way. *But:*

(a) In this sense the value of a commodity is taken to mean its price.

(b) The term "value" as applied to money may mean:

(i) What money will buy, that is, the purchasing power of money, or

(ii) The price of money, that is, the rate of interest.

18. The supply of money. This can be defined in two ways:

(a) Notes and coin together with bank deposits on current account, this amount sometimes being represented by the symbol M^1.

(b) M^1 together with deposits on deposit account at both banks and discount houses, this amount being represented as M^3 (the term M^2 is no longer in use).

In 1975 M^1 stood at £13,325 million with M^3 at £33,604 million.

19. The demand for money and liquidity-preference. There is, too, a difference between the demand for a commodity which is wanted for its own sake and the demand for money, which is defined as the demand to hold money as distinct from investing it. Thus, an increase in the demand for money is an increase in the preference for liquidity, just as a decrease in the demand for money means a decline in liquidity-preference.

Liquidity-preference, therefore, is the indicator of the strength of the demand for money.

20. The three influences on the demand for money. Lord Keynes distinguished three motives for holding money:

(a) The transactions motive.

(b) The precautionary motive.

(c) The speculative motive.

21. The transactions motive. It is necessary for people to keep money available for their ordinary routine expenditure to cover such items as food, clothing, rent (or payments to a building society), fuel and light, drink, tobacco, etc. The amount each person requires for this purpose depends on:

(a) The time interval between each pay-day; the longer the interval the greater the amount required.

(b) His standard of living.

(c) The size of his income.

22. The precautionary motive. Most people prefer to hold rather more than the minimum necessary for the transactions motive as a reserve against unforeseen contingencies, such as price increases, household repairs and renewals, or sickness.

23. The speculative motive. The demand for money for the transactions and precautionary motives will be fairly stable in the short period (unless it is one of severe inflation). Short-term changes in the demand for money are, therefore, mainly due to the speculative motive. The cost of holding money instead of investing it is the interest it would otherwise earn.

It is advantageous to hold money instead of investing it if the investor thinks that in the near future the prevailing rate of interest is likely to rise, that is, the capital value of assets is likely to fall. For example, if one could foresee a fall in the price of a 6 per cent Government stock from £60 to £54 in six months it would be advantageous to postpone its purchase, for the loss of interest for six months would be only £3, whereas the gain on the purchase price would be £6. In other words, the gain from postponement of investment is due to a rise in the rate of interest (or rate of yield) from 10 per cent to 11 per cent.

24. A second equation of exchange. The following equation of exchange has been constructed to take account of the demand for money:

$$p = \frac{M}{kR}$$

The symbols represent:

M = the supply of money (as in the quantity equation);
R = the real income or volume of production—somewhat similar to T of the other equation;
k = the proportion of the national income that people prefer to hold in the form of money, that is, the demand for money (*cf.* V of the quantity equation);
p = the price level of consumers' goods, whereas P in the other equation represents the *general* price level.

RATE OF INTEREST

25. The nature of interest. Interest is a payment for a service—for the use of money. It can, therefore, be regarded as the price of money—a charge to be paid for borrowing money.

There are three elements in gross interest:

(*a*) A payment for the trouble involved in making the loan.

(b) A payment for the risk involved; the greater the risk the greater the amount to be paid.

(c) Pure interest, that is, the actual charge for the use of the money.

26. The importance of interest.

(a) It affects the development of and expansion of economic activity.

(b) It influences the holding of stocks by wholesalers, whose costs rise if the rate of interest is increased.

(c) It influences the rate of saving, more generally being saved when the rate of interest is low (*see* XIII, **5** below).

27. The rate of yield. The prevailing rate of interest is the rate at which different classes of borrowers can borrow at a particular time. What that rate is can be seen from the current rate of yield on existing stocks and shares. Thus, when 6 per cent funding loan, 1993, stood at $42\frac{1}{2}$ in 1975 the interest yield was over 14 per cent. This means that if the Government wished to issue a new stock with similar dates of redemption it would have to offer about 14 per cent to attract investors.

28. Theories of interest. Many theories have been put forward to explain the determination of the rate of interest. Consider the following:

(a) The time-preference theory. Some people prefer to have the use of a smaller sum of money now rather than a larger sum at some time in the future, whilst other prefers a larger sum in the future to a smaller sum now. In other words, one prefers to pay interest to have the use of a sum of money now while the others prefer to receive interest to forgo the use of his money until a future date. The equilibrium (or natural) rate of interest equates the supply of loanable funds with the demand for them.

(b) The marginal productivity theory. According to this theory the rate of interest depends on a "real" influence—the productivity of real capital. An entrepreneur will borrow money for the purchase of new capital equipment only if he expects that the return on this new capital will at least equal the rate of interest he has to pay on the loan.

(c) The monetary theory. Since the demand for money depends on expectations of changes in the rate of interest it will require a high rate of interest to induce people to part with liquidity if their liquidity-preference is strong. Thus, the

rate of interest is determined by their attitude towards liquidity. Lord Keynes considered the rate of interest to be the "reward for parting with liquidity for a period."

29. The short-term and long-term rates of interest. The *short-term rate of interest* is indicated by the yield on Treasury bills and stock exchange securities that are nearing maturity, that is, with only a year or so to run.

The *long-term rate* is indicated by the yield on long-dated Government securities, such as $5\frac{1}{2}$ per cent Treasury Stock, 2008–12, and unredeemable stocks such as $2\frac{1}{2}$ per cent Consols.

(a) The long-term and short-term rates of interest influence one another. Generally, the long-term rate of interest is higher than the short-term, since the longer the period the greater the risk, and the two rates tend to move up and down together, for speculators will switch about between long-term and short-term securities whenever it is to their advantage to do so.

(b) However, when interest rates generally are high, as in 1973–75, some longer-term rates may be lower than short-term rates because the very high rates of interest are not expected to persist for long.

Since the long-term rate is made up of a series of short-term rates it has been argued that this is the *fundamental rate.* Lord Keynes, however, believed that Bank rate made its influence felt through the long-term rate.

CHAPTER XI

THE IMPORTANCE OF CHANGES IN THE VALUE OF MONEY

PRICES AND PRODUCTION

1. Economic effects of price changes. Changes in the value of money (that is, changes in prices) have two important economic consequences:

(*a*) They influence the level of production (*see* **2** below).
(*b*) They influence the distribution of the national income (*see* **4** below).

These are examples of the dynamic function of money.

2. Falling prices and production. When prices are falling the risks of the entrepreneur are increased. In these conditions the price at which the product can eventually be marketed will be less than that expected when its production was first undertaken.

Thus, even the entrepreneur who fairly accurately forecasts his costs of production will make less profit than he originally anticipated. An entrepreneur who finds that his costs turn out to be higher than he expected may make little or no profit or incur a loss as a result of the fall in price. The reason for this is that although the prices of final products may fall quite sharply some costs of production change only slowly or not at all. Since falling prices increase entrepreneurial risk, entrepreneurs tend to be more cautious in these conditions and curtail their output.

Thus with falling prices production too tends to fall and unemployment increases. As a result, total demand falls off, and a further increase in unemployment occurs and production declines still further.

On account of its bad effect on production and employment deflation came to be regarded as a policy to be avoided.

3. Rising prices and production. The effect of rising prices is to stimulate production and reduce unemployment. In these conditions the price at which a product can be marketed will be higher than was expected. Consequently, profit margins will be widened and entrepreneurs will be encouraged to expand their output, thereby increasing production, reducing unemployment and expanding demand.

A mildly inflationary condition, therefore, seems to be advantageous to production.

PRICES AND DISTRIBUTION

4. Effect of price changes on distribution. The effect of a change in the value of money is an arbitrary redistribution of incomes because different groups of people are differently affected:

(a) People with fixed incomes. Those whose incomes are fixed in terms of money will clearly be better off when prices are falling and worse off when prices are rising. In this group are retired people who derive their incomes from fixed pensions or past savings invested in fixed-interest securities. However, many pensions, including the State retirement pension, have come to be adjusted at intervals, though there is usually a time lag of four to six months.

(b) People with incomes from profits. These people generally gain when prices are rising because their incomes tend to rise more than prices. When, however, prices are falling their incomes generally fall to a greater extent than prices.

(c) Earners of wages and salaries.

(i) Wage-earners in the past often found that a time-lag occurred between a change in prices and an adjustment of wages, so that when prices were rising their real wages fell slightly but fewer people were out of work; but when prices were falling, although real wages rose slightly, unemployment increased. In the prolonged period of inflation that has existed since 1945, wages eventually forged ahead of price increases.

(ii) Salary-earners. In the past salary-earners tended to be classed with people on fixed incomes, so that they were worse off when prices were rising and better off when prices were falling. Since 1955, however, salaries have generally tended to keep pace with rising prices and more recently, like wages, gone ahead of price rises.

INFLATION

5. Types of inflation. Inflation can take any one of three forms:

(a) Inflation on the gold standard. This is nothing more than the moderate and controlled expansion of credit that occurs on the gold standard whenever there is an inflow of gold.

(b) Persistent inflation. Also known as "creeping" inflation, this is a condition where the volume of purchasing power is persistently running ahead of the supply of both commodities and factors of production (especially labour). As a result there is a persistent tendency for prices and wages to rise.

(i) Demand inflation. This is a persistent inflation where the inflationary spiral of prices and wages is induced by an excess of demand over supply—the result either of an excessive creation of purchasing power or of a curtailment of supply (as in time of war).

(ii) Cost inflation. This occurs when the inflationary spiral is induced by increase costs—generally higher wages.

(c) Hyperinflation. Also known as a "galloping" or "runaway" inflation, this is the most serious kind. Prices rise at an ever-increasing rate until huge sums of money have to be paid for quite cheap things. In the later stages the value of money declines rapidly from day to day until it becomes almost worthless and a new currency has to be introduced.

If inflation persists over a long period (as it has since 1945) it tends to get worse at an increasing rate. There is always a danger, therefore, that a persistent inflation may degenerate into a hyperinflation if it is not effectively controlled.

6. Effects of inflation. The following are some of the likely effects of a hyperinflation:

(a) At first real capital investment may be stimulated.

(b) If there was unemployment at the onset of the inflation this will generally disappear. During 1973–75 there was the paradoxical situation of both inflation and unemployment increasing together.

Sometimes, therefore, the immediate effects have appeared good, but in the past a hyperinflation has taken the following course:

(c) Real capital investment will be checked because of insufficient resources to meet the demand for it.

(d) Shortages of labour will arise in most industries.

(e) Prices will then begin to rise steeply, and increases in wages will follow.

(f) Savings will be discouraged.

(g) Goods will come to be preferred to money balances.

(h) The velocity of circulation of money will increase as people become less willing to hold money.

(i) There will be increasing difficulty with the balance of payments as the prices of exports rise.

(j) Loss of confidence in the monetary unit will lead to the use of some other unit of account, possibly a more stable foreign currency or even a commodity.

(k) Eventually it may be necessary to introduce a new monetary unit probably equal in value to a huge amount of the discredited currency unit.

(l) People whose savings were in any form of monetary investment — bank deposits, Government stocks, debentures — will find them almost worthless. Debtors will gain, but creditors will lose.

7. Causes of inflation. The following circumstances may provide the environment in which inflation can arise:

(a) In time of war:

(i) When an increase in the volume of purchasing power occurs in the production of goods for war purposes but not available to consumers.

(ii) When there is a shortage of consumers' goods.

(iii) There is likely to be an "inflationary gap," that is, an excess of Government expenditure over Government income, covered either by borrowing from the banks through the issue of Treasury bills (the usual British method) or by the printing of new money.

(b) In post-war conditions when the shortage of consumers' goods is still likely to persist and people wish to spend money saved during the war.

(c) A currency deliberately ruined by a government that wishes to reduce its external obligations, especially if these take the form of reparations imposed after losing a war, as with Germany in 1922–23.

(d) A government unwilling to balance its budget by an unpopular increase in taxation will have to cover the deficit by having recourse to inflationary borrowing, as a result of which there will be an increase in the money supply.

(e) Government responsibility for full employment:

(i) Making certain of full employment by stimulating demand will usually result in over-full employment, with a greater demand for labour than the supply. An attempt to secure an over-rapid increase in the rate of economic growth will have a similar result.

(ii) Trade unions are likely to press repeated demands for wage increases and in these conditions their demands are likely to be met.

(iii) The longer the period of full employment the more militant the trade unions tend to become and the greater their demands, so that increases in wages occur unaccompanied by a corresponding increase in productivity and output.

8. Examples of hyperinflation.

(a) After the First World War: Germany, Austria, Russia, Poland.

(b) After the Second World War: Hungary, Rumania, Greece, China.

(c) Since 1960: Brazil, Argentina, Chile.

CHAPTER XII

MONEY AND INDUSTRIAL FLUCTUATIONS

FEATURES OF INDUSTRIAL FLUCTUATIONS

1. Periods of industrial fluctuation.

(a) From 1792 to 1913. The term "trade (or business cycle" is generally restricted to the industrial fluctuations that occurred during this period.

(b) From 1919 to 1939. The feature of the period between the two World Wars was a prolonged trade depression. During 1926-29 it mainly affected Great Britain, being the result of the deflationary policy consequent on returning to the gold standard at the pre-1914 parity. After 1929 the depression became world-wide.

(c) Since 1945. The outstanding feature of this period was the high level of employment that was almost continuously maintained until the recession of 1975.

2. The nineteenth-century trade cycle. The main features of the trade cycle were:

(a) Trade booms and trade depressions alternated with one another, with intervals of seven or eight years between each boom and the next.

(b) Both booms and depressions were of short duration.

(c) The upswing of the cycle was characterised by:

(i) Expanding demand.
(ii) Increasing production.
(iii) Building up of merchants' stocks.
(iv) Falling unemployment.
(v) Rising prices, wage and profits, *i.e.* falling value of money.
(vi) Expanding foreign trade.
(vii) An increase of bank credit and the supply of money.

(d) The downswing of the cycle was characterised by:

(i) Declining demand.
(ii) Falling production.
(iii) The running down of merchants' stocks.
(iv) Rising unemployment.
(v) Falling prices, wages and profits, *i.e.* increasing value of money.
(vi) Declining foreign trade.
(vii) A contraction of bank credit and a reduction in the supply of money.

(e) The first industries to be affected in both boom and slump are the capital-producing industries. These industries experience, too, the greatest extremes of prosperity and depression.

(f) The course of the cycle was as follows:

(i) The upswing—a period of expanding activity.
(ii) The peak of the boom.
(iii) The downswing—a period of declining activity.
(iv) The bottom of the depression.

IRREGULARITY OF RECENT FLUCTUATIONS

3. Between the two World Wars. A brief post-war boom in 1920–21 was followed by the Great Depression. After 1935 it appeared as if the trade cycle might re-assert itself, but with "booms" below the level of full employment. The main features of the Great Depression were:

(a) It was of much longer duration than the depressions associated with the nineteenth-century trade cycle.

(b) It was also much more severe than any previous depression, with very high rates of unemployment, especially in areas of highly localised industries.

(c) The trade unions were stronger than formerly and in consequence wages in manufacturing industry proved to be "sticky," with the result that wage rates fell less than they otherwise might, but unemployment was heavier in these industries.

(d) World prices of raw materials and foodstuffs fell to very low levels. As a result, farmers' incomes were greatly reduced but unemployment was less severe than in manufacturing industry.

(e) There was a "chronic deficiency of demand," as Lord Beveridge showed.

(f) A greater proportion of "black-coated" workers were affected (especially in the United States) than in previous depressions.

(g) On account of its world-wide character a greater number of countries than ever before were led to adopt short-sighted economic policies, the effect of which was to reduce the volume of world trade still further.

4. The period since 1945. The outstanding feature of this period has been almost continuous full employment.

(a) Definitions of full employment:

(i) A condition where "there are more jobs than men" (Lord Beveridge). Such a condition would ensure full employment, but in these circumstances it would be impossible to avoid inflation.

(ii) A condition where the number of people unemployed does not exceed the number of vacancies, the unemployment that would occur in this case being merely the result of lack of complete mobility of labour.

(b) Over-full employment. It follows, therefore, from definition *(ii)* above that there is over-full employment when the number of vacancies exceeds the number of people unemployed, that is, when the demand for labour exceeds the supply. This is a characteristic of inflation.

Since the maintenance of full employment has become a political question, governments tend to over-stimulate production, so that over-full employment results.

5. Recent fluctuations.

(a) A modified form of the trade cycle, however, has been discernible, with brief periods of over-full employment alternating with equally brief periods of mild recession as in 1952–53, 1958–59, 1962–63, 1966–69. The recessions were generally the result of disinflationary measures taken to check inflation after full employment had developed from measures taken to check recession ("stop-go" policies). More serious unemployment occurred in 1975–65.

(b) Throughout the period there was a general tendency for prices and wages to rise, that is, for the value of money to fall, as a result of persistent inflation. During 1968–74, in spite of rising unemployment, credit restriction and exceptionally high interest rates, prices and wages rose more rapidly. This round of inflation was set in motion by the devaluation of sterling in 1967.

CAUSES OF THE TRADE CYCLE

6. A multiplicity of causes. Many different theories have been put forward to explain the trade cycle, some emphasising real causes and others stressing monetary influences. In fact, there were probably three groups of causes:

(a) Real causes.
(b) Psychological causes.
(c) Monetary causes.

7. Real causes.

(a) The economic system—production, distribution and exchange—has become increasingly complex and uncertainty has increased.

(b) Economic progress tends to be irregular, periods of rapid technological improvement alternating with periods of a slower rate of change.

(c) The demand for capital goods tends to be irregular. The demand for capital goods is derived from the demand for the consumers' goods in the production of which they are required. Fluctuations in the demand for consumers' goods instigate even wider fluctuations in the demand for capital goods.

(d) Irregularity of output occurs in agriculture, partly as a result of vagaries of the weather and partly on account of the slowness of the response of supply to price changes.

8. Psychological causes. According to this theory, fluctuations in economic activity depend primarily on the confidence of business men in the future:

(a) If they consider that a depression is not likely to last much longer, they may decide to renew capital equipment while prices are low, thereby stimulating recovery. If they expect rising prices to continue they will expand production.

(b) If a boom has developed and they do not think it likely to continue they may postpone renewal of capital equipment, thereby hastening the end of the boom. If they expect prices to fall they will curtail production.

Lord Keynes stressed the influence of "expectations" on the actions of entrepreneurs and investors.

PURELY MONETARY THEORIES

9. Variations in bank credit. When production is expanding, it is said, there is an increased demand for bank loans and, since lending is their most profitable activity, there is in consequence a tendency for an over-expansion of bank credit to occur. After a boom has developed, fear of inflation then leads banks to contract credit, with the result that the boom is brought to an end.

There is no doubt that booms and depressions are associated respectively with expansion and contraction of bank credit, but critics of this theory assert that changes in bank credit policy are a *consequence* and not a *cause* of the trade cycle.

10. Variations in the rate of interest. A distinction can be made between a natural rate and a market rate of interest:

(a) *The natural rate* is that which equates the demand for loans with the supply of loanable funds.

(b) *The market rate* is the actual rate at which banks are prepared to lend at a particular time.

An over-expansion of bank credit then occurs whenever the market rate falls below the natural rate.

11. The rate of interest and the holding of stocks. Some writers believe that it is through its effect on the holding of stocks that the rate of interest makes its influence felt. A rise in interest rates increases the cost of holding stocks and so merchants allow their stocks to run down, with the result that manufacturers have to curtail production. A reduction in the rate of interest, therefore, encourages the building up of stocks and stimulates production (*see also* **14** below).

UNDER-CONSUMPTION THEORIES

12. Loss of purchasing power. The cruder versions of under-consumption theory suggest that in a modern economic system there is a permanent tendency for purchasing power to fall short of the amount required to purchase all the goods and services produced, that is, that purchasing power is lost. Supporters of this theory, therefore, believe that the remedy lies in the State's periodically supplementing consumers' purchasing power.

It is, however, a fallacy to assume that purchasing power is lost, since all the *costs* of production become *income* to those receiving payment. If an article is bought for 60p this may include a payment of 20p for the retailer's services, and perhaps 10p to the wholesaler, the rest being the manufacturer's costs (rent, wages, interest) and his profit, all these being income to those receiving them.

13. Over-saving. This theory suggests that inequality of incomes leads to too much saving, so that over-investment occurs. Over-production of capital goods is not, however, a feature of a depression.

14. The structure of production and the rate of interest. The effect of a low rate of interest, some writers believe, is to lengthen the structure of production by making it more "roundabout," that is, introducing more stages of production and more specialisation.

Thus, encouraged by the low rate of interest, there is over-investment in the later stages of a boom, and some projects may have to be abandoned when the downswing of the cycle occurs.

15. Saving-investment theory. This forms part of the theory of income determination which is dealt with in the next chapter.

CHAPTER XIII

SAVING, INVESTMENT AND INCOME

DEFINITIONS OF TERMS

1. Types of production. There are two main types of production:

(a) The production of *consumers'* goods.
(b) The production of *producers'* goods.

The aim of production is to satisfy the wants of consumers, individually or collectively. Producers' goods (or capital goods) —factories, machinery, means of transport—are required only because they assist the further production of consumers' goods.

2. The national income. This can be regarded from two angles:

(a) The money value of all goods and services produced during a period—the volume of production.
(b) The total of all incomes derived from economic activity.

Either method will yield the same money total, since the total costs of production become income—rent, wages, interest and profit—to those engaged in production.

3. Investment. This means, in real terms, the actual production of capital goods. Investment may be:

(a) Private, as when a firm installs a new machine.
(b) Public, as when the State builds a new road.

The amount of investment determines the volume of consumers' goods that can be produced. Investment, therefore, is the most important influence on the size of the national income and so of individual incomes.

4. Consumption. This is the quantity or the money value of all consumers' goods purchased during a period.

5. Saving. Economically, anything that reduces the demand for consumers' goods can be regarded as saving:

(a) Voluntary saving by individuals or companies. The rate of interest is the monetary inducement to save, though much saving is independent of the rate of interest. Nevertheless, saving is greater when the rate of interest is high than when it is low.

(b) Compulsory "saving" as a result of taxation.

(c) "Forced saving" following a rise in prices unaccompanied by any increase in income.

6. Saving and investment.

(a) In real terms, saving must be sufficient to release factors of production from the production of consumers' goods to enable them to be employed on the production of producers' goods.

(b) In money terms, the value of total saving must be sufficient to finance real capital investment.

Thus saving is a necessary precursor of investment.

PSYCHOLOGICAL INFLUENCES

7. The propensity to save. This is the keenness of people to save. In only a few cases is it related to the need for investment, as when part of the profits of a business (sole proprietor, partnership or company) is used to finance expansion.

In most cases the saving of individuals is totally unrelated to the needs of investment.

An important influence on the propensity to save is the general level of incomes.

8. The propensity to consume. This is the keenness of people to spend on consumers' goods. It is influenced by the general level of economic activity, the level of personal income and the outlook for the future.

The marginal propensity to consume is greater for people with low incomes than for those with high incomes.

9. Expectations. The amount of investment undertaken by entrepreneurs depends on their expectations of the future level of economic activity. If they expect a high level of business activity to be maintained they will be keen to increase investment, but if they fear a recession this will check investment.

10. The marginal efficiency of capital. Another important influence on investment is the relation between the rate of interest (the cost to a business of borrowing) and the *expected* yield on a new item of investment. An entrepreneur will install a new machine only if the expected additional profit resulting from its employment at least equals the interest that will have to be paid on the sum borrowed for its purchase.

Thus £2,000 would be borrowed at 10 per cent to buy a new machine only if it was expected to yield at least £200 per annum.

DETERMINATION OF INCOME

11. The main factors in income determination.

(*a*) Investment generates income.
(*b*) Income determines the level of saving.
(*c*) Income also determines the level of consumption.
(*d*) Saving is a necessary pre-requisite for investment.
(*e*) Consumption also stimulates investment.

Thus, income, investment, saving and consumption are all dependent on one another.

12. The multiplier. Investment—whether undertaken by the State or the private sector of industry—costing (say) £2 million will yield income of the same amount to all those directly concerned with its production. These increases in income, however, will stimulate consumers' demand for other things, the production of which will increase total income still further.

Not all the income resulting from the new investment will be spent. Allowing for saving, perhaps £1.8 million might be spent at this second round, thus adding a further £1.8 to total income.

At each successive round the addition to total income will become smaller, so that eventually the effect of the new investment dies out. This is known as the *multiplier effect.* If total income has been increased by £6 million as a result of an original investment of £2 million the *multiplier* is 3.

The multiplier effect can also be considered in terms of employment. If the original investment provides work for 3,000 men, the increase in demand may eventually result in work for 9,000 men. Again the multiplier is 3

13. Other factors in income determination.

(a) Investment is influenced by:

(i) Expectations.
(ii) The marginal efficiency of capital.
(iii) The rate of interest, which is influenced by:
1. The quantity of money.
2. Liquidity-preference.

(b) Saving is influenced by:

(i) The propensity to save.
(ii) The level of income.
(iii) The rate of interest.

(c) Consumption is influenced by:

(i) The propensity to consume.
(ii) The level of income.

(d) Income is influenced by:

(i) Investment.
(ii) Saving.
(iii) Consumption.

Finally:

(e) Employment is influenced by:

(i) Investment.
(ii) Consumption.

SAVING AND INVESTMENT

14. Two points of view. There are two theories of the relationship between saving and investment:

(a) Differences in the levels of saving and investment are the causes of depressions and inflationary booms:

(i) When saving exceeds investment a depression occurs, demand being insufficient to employ the entire labour supply.

(ii) When investment exceeds saving an inflationary boom occurs, the demand for labour exceeding the supply.

According to this theory, equilibrium occurs when saving and investment are equal.

(b) Saving and investment are always equal, and this can occur at different levels of employment—the Keynesian theory.

15. Equality of saving and investment. Lord Keynes demonstrated this as follows:

(a) The national income can be regarded as the total of all incomes derived from economic activity, and since income is either spent or saved, then:

$$\text{Income} = \text{Saving} + \text{Consumption}$$

Therefore:

$$\text{Saving} = \text{Income} - \text{Consumption}$$

(b) The national income can also be regarded as the total volume of production, and since production consists of producers' goods (investment) and consumers' goods, then:

$$\text{Income} = \text{Investment} + \text{Consumption}$$

Therefore:

$$\text{Investment} = \text{Income} - \text{Consumption}$$

(c) Since both saving and investment are each equal to Income minus Consumption they must, therefore, be equal to one another.

16. The "period" analysis. For a long time controversy raged over the two theories of saving and investment. Attempts made by several writers to reconcile them have been by the "period" analysis.

The saving and consumption that occur in one period depend on the income and investment of the previous period. Thus, it is the amount of investment of the first period that generates an equal amount of saving in the second period. In this way saving and investment are equal, although they may not necessarily be so at any particular time.

CHAPTER XIV

MONETARY POLICY

AIMS OF MONETARY POLICY

1. The dynamic function of money. Whatever instruments may be employed to carry it out, the purpose of monetary policy is to influence the supply of money in order to expand or contract the volume of purchasing power in the country.

An increase in the volume of purchasing power is expected to stimulate demand and investment, increase output and reduce unemployment. A reduction in the supply of money would be expected to have exactly the opposite effects.

2. Types of policy.

(a) Inflation—an expansion of the monetary supply (on the gold standard inflation was strictly controlled).

(b) Deflation—a contraction of the monetary supply.

(c) Disinflation—a mild form of deflation which since the 1930s had come to be associated with depression.

(d) Reflation—a mild form of inflation.

3. Government policy today.

(a) Internal aim:

(i) To maintain full employment.

(ii) To stimulate economic growth, that is, an expansion of the real national income.

(iii) To keep inflation in check.

(b) External aim: To keep the balance of payments in balance and maintain the value of sterling abroad. When a currency is linked to gold this involves protecting the country's gold and convertible currency reserves.

4. Conflict of aims. The above aims often conflict with one another:

(a) Full employment and inflation. Anxiety on the part of the Government to maintain full employment at all times for political reasons and inability to calculate the precise amount of investment that will give full employment results in over-investment and over-full employment.

(b) Inflation and economic growth. A policy aiming to

check inflation will tend also to check economic growth, especially if a bout of severe inflation has been allowed to develop so that disinflationary measures have had to be adopted.

(c) The balance of payments and internal policy. An internal expansionist policy either to stimulate economic growth (rising prices stimulate production) or to reduce unemployment will increase the demand for imports both of consumers' goods and raw materials. As a result, a deficit in the balance of payments is likely to occur and, if large and persistent, the external value of sterling will be threatened.

Nevertheless, the internal and external situations very often require the same policy. Clearly, a disinflationary policy will be advantageous both internally and externally when difficulties with the balance of payments are the consequence of internal inflation.

TECHNIQUES OF MONETARY POLICY

The following are instruments of monetary policy that have been employed in Great Britain:

5. The traditional instruments of policy.

(a) Bank rate (Minimum lending rate and base rate since 1971–72).

(b) Open-market operations.

6. Modern instruments of policy.

(a) The Treasury directive.

(b) Special deposits.

7. Adjuncts to monetary policy.

(a) Fiscal policy—budgeting for a surplus or a deficit.

(b) "The regulator"—variations (since 1975 up to 25 per cent) by Order in Council in indirect taxes such as VAT, tobacco and petrol duties.

(c) Variation of hire-purchase regulations. Following the recommendation of the *Crowther Report* (1971) this instrument of policy has not been employed.

8. Alternative to monetary policy. Physical controls—rationing, licensing of raw materials, import quotas, exchange control.

THE TRADITIONAL INSTRUMENTS OF POLICY

9. Bank rate (*see* also IV, **10**). This was the minimum rate at which the Bank of England would re-discount first class or bank bills. Until 1971–72 its importance lay in other interest rates being linked to it:

(a) directly—the lending rate of the commercial banks and the rate these banks pay on deposit accounts;

(b) indirectly—the rate at which the Government and local authorities can borrow, and also in the long run the rates of building societies.

10. The theory of interest rate changes. As an instrument of monetary policy, changes in interest rates make borrowing cheaper or dearer.

(a) When interest rates are low (*i.e.* when money is "cheap") it may be expected that more will be borrowed, and so an expansion of purchasing power will take place, stimulating demand and encouraging an increase in output and in imports. If, however, rates are lower in London than in other financial centres, there may be a tendency for foreign holders of sterling to transfer funds to centres where a higher rate of interest prevails.

(b) When interest rates are high money is said to be dear and less borrowing may be expected, so that production will be checked and the volume of purchasing power reduced, thereby checking demand and so tending to cause a further fall in output and in imports. High interest rates in London will tend to attract more funds from abroad.

11. Open-market operations (*see* also IV, **7,8**).

(a) By intervention on the stock exchange through its broker, the Bank of England can influence the cash reserves and, therefore, the liquidity of the commercial banks (*see* IV, **8**). The aim too is to influence the short-term and the long-term rates of interest.

(b) Objections to open-market operations:

(i) They are a clumsy device.

(ii) If banks maintain excess reserves they become immune from this method of control by the central bank.

(c) Alternatives to open-market operations:

(i) Varying the legal cash ratio, as in the United States.
(ii) The Treasury directive, as used in Great Britain.
(iii) Special deposits, as used in Great Britain.

12. Efficacy of Bank rate.

(a) Before 1914. During the nineteenth century the Bank of England regarded Bank rate as its primary instrument of monetary policy, open-market operations being employed only to make Bank rate "effective." Some later writers disagree with this view.

(b) Between the two world wars. Bank rate became discredited. It was said that

(i) In a great depression even a very low Bank rate would not stimulate recovery.

(ii) A high Bank rate would not check a boom when profits were very high.

From 1932 to 1951 Bank rate was kept unchanged at 2 per cent, except for a brief temporary change in 1939.

(c) 1951–72. Bank rate was revived as an instrument of monetary policy because other methods used to check inflation had failed. Between 1951 and 1972, Bank rate varied between $2\frac{1}{2}$ per cent and 8 per cent. During this period Bank rate was always employed in conjunction with other instruments—a policy that came to be known as the "package deal" (*see* XVI, **6***(d)*).

OTHER INSTRUMENTS OF POLICY

13. The Treasury directive. This was an instruction from the Treasury to the banks to restrict credit. It took two forms:

(a) The qualitative directive. Advances were to be restricted to purposes "in the national interest"—an impossible condition to impose on a banker.

(b) The quantitative directive. Advances were to be restricted irrespective of the purpose for which they were required.

14. Special deposits. The Bank of England can call upon the commercial banks to deposit with it a specified fraction of their total deposits (usually 1 per cent or 2 per cent), these deposits being "frozen" until released by the monetary authorities. Such deposits, unlike bankers' deposits, bear interest but cannot be regarded as part of the commercial banks' cash reserves, which are thereby reduced, thus compelling these banks to reduce their deposits by curtailing their lending.

15. Fiscal policy. The changing *character and purpose* of the budget:

(a) Until the twentieth century the main concern of the Chancellor of the Exchequer was to ensure that just sufficient revenue was raised as was necessary to cover expenditure on administration, defence and the maintenance of law and order.

(b) As the State undertook the supply of an increasing number of social and welfare services, revenue had to be raised to cover expenditure for these purposes.

(c) The budget is now used to reduce inequality of income through steeply progressive taxation.

(d) Since 1947 a large budget surplus has been used as a means of reducing the volume of purchasing in order to check inflation. The drawback to this policy is that it requires taxation to be at a high level, and this can be a disincentive to production. A budget deficit, it has been suggested, might be used to stimulate recovery from a depression.

(e) Variations in indirect taxes, especially purchase taxes, and VAT, have been made either *(i)* to check demand (by increasing such taxes), or *(ii)* to stimulate demand to promote recovery from a recession (by reducing these taxes).

16. Hire-purchase. The huge expansion since 1945 of hire-purchase in Great Britain made changes in the amount of such business of considerable economic importance. The State took action with regard to hire-purchase in two ways:

(a) By varying the amount of the initial deposit.

(b) By varying the maximum period of repayment. To check inflation the minimum deposit could be increased and the period of repayment reduced. To encourage recovery from a recession the minimum deposit could be reduced and the period of repayment lengthened.

Advantage. Changes in hire purchase regulations were quick to take effect, since most people who make use of hire-purchase appear to be more concerned with the amount of the immediate payments than with the ultimate cost of the article.

Disadvantage. Only those industries producing goods mainly sold by this method—more expensive durable goods—were affected, and on them the effect was severe.

On account of these disadvantages the *Crowther Report* (1971) recommended that hire purchase should not be regarded as an instrument of monetary policy. Since then, it has not been employed.

PROGRESS TEST 3

MONEY AS A DYNAMIC FACTOR

1. Consider the importance of money as a measure of value. (X, **2**)
2. Distinguish between the "value of money" and the "price of money." (X, **3, 4**)
3. There has been a long-period tendency for the value of money to fall. Why, therefore, are we so concerned about the fall in the value of money at the present day? (X, **6**)
4. Do you regard the index of retail prices as a satisfactory means of measuring the value of money? (X, **10, 11**)
5. Enunciate the quantity theory of money. What are the main criticisms that have been levelled against it? (X, **12, 15, 16**)
6. Explain the meaning of the following:*(a)* the demand for money, *(b)* liquidity-preference, *(c)* velocity of circulation. (X, **13, 14, 19**)
7. Since it is an expense to hold money, why then do people hold money? (X, **20**)
8. Distinguish between the rate of interest and the rate of yield. (X, **26, 27**)
9. What is the economic importance of interest? (X, **26**)
10. What determines the prevailing rate of interest at a particular time? (X, **28**)
11. Consider the connection between the short-term and the long-term rates of interest. (X, **29**)
12. What would be *(a)* the advantages and *(b)* the disadvantages of a persistent fall in the value of money? (XI, **2, 4**)
13. "Inflation is a bad thing." "There are beneficial effects of rising prices." Can you reconcile these two statements? (XI,**1-3, 4, 6**)
14. Explain the following terms: *(a)* persistent inflation; *(b)* demand inflation; *(c)* cost inflation; *(d)* hyperinflation. (XI, **5**)
15. Show how inflation can arise. What factors tend to make it persist? (XI, **7**)
16. If the quantity of money were to be doubled would all prices double? (X, **12-16**)
17. Compare the industrial fluctuations of the three periods: *(a)* before 1913; *(b)* 1919-39; *(c)* since 1945. (XII, **1, 2**)
18. What were the main features of the upswing and downswing of the trade cycle during the nineteenth century? (XII, **2**)
19. In what ways did the Great Depression (1929-35) differ from the pre-1913 depressions? (XII, **3**)
20. Define full employment. (XII, **5**)

21. What do you understand by over-full employment? (XII, **5**)

22. In what sense was the trade cycle due to "a multiplicity of causes"? (XII, **6**)

23. How far do you think monetary influences were responsible for the trade cycle? (XII, **9-11**)

24. Distinguish between *(a)* the market rate and *(b)* the natural rate of interest. (XII, **10**)

25. Discuss the under-consumption theories of the trade cycle. (XII, **12, 13**)

26. Give two definitions of the national income. Can they be reconciled? (XIII, **2**)

27. Define the terms: *(a)* saving, *(b)* investment. (XIII, **3, 5**)

28. Consider Lord Keynes's "psychological influences." (XIII, **7-9**)

29. Explain "the marginal efficiency of capital." (XIII, **10**)

30. What is the multiplier? (XIII, **12**)

31. Show how investment, saving and consumption are related to one another. (XIII, **13**)

32. Is it possible to reconcile *(c)* the view that in a depression saving is greater than investment with *(b)* Lord Keynes's view that saving and investment are always equal? If so, how? (XIII, **15**)

33. What do you understand by the dynamic function of money? (XIV, **1**)

34. What are the main aims of monetary policy? (XIV, **2, 3**)

35. Is full employment possible without inflation? (XIV, **4**)

36. What are the main checks to economic growth in Great Britain at the present time? (XIV, **4**)

37. "The difficulty in deciding what type of monetary policy to pursue is that both the internal and external interests of a country have to be considered." Discuss this statement. (XIV, **4**)

38. Compare the efficacy of Bank rate and the newer instruments of monetary policy—the Treasury directive and special deposits. (XIV, **8, 9, 10**)

39. Describe the theory of Bank rate changes. (XIV, **9**)

40. What was the purpose of the Treasury directive? Distinguish between a "qualitative" and a "quantitative" directive. (XIV, **13**)

41. What are special deposits? For what purpose have they been employed? (XIV, **14**)

42. In what ways can fiscal policy be employed as an adjunct to monetary policy? (XIV, **15**)

PART FOUR

RECENT MONETARY DEVELOPMENTS

CHAPTER XV

SOME MONETARY PROBLEMS OF THE POST-WAR PERIOD (1945-51)

THE AMERICAN LOAN (1945)

1. Great Britain's need to borrow.

(a) The Bretton Woods scheme could not be put fully into operation until member countries had recovered somewhat from the effects of the war. A transition period of five years was anticipated.

(b) The Second World War placed a heavy burden on Great Britain, which had been a belligerent for a longer period than any other country:

(i) Many foreign investments had been sold.

(ii) Its gold reserves had been depleted.

(iii) Its economy had been geared almost entirely to the needs of the war.

(iv) Its export trade had almost ceased.

(v) Severe shipping losses had been suffered.

(vi) There had been heavy capital consumption, mainly as a result of failure to make good depreciation and to some extent of enemy action.

(c) For some time, therefore, Great Britain had to import on credit both food and raw materials until its industries had been reorganised for peacetime production and goods produced for export.

2. The Washington Loan Agreement, 1945.

(a) The financial terms were not onerous:

(i) The United States was to allow Great Britain a line of credit of $3,750 million.

(ii) Interest at a rate of only 2 per cent was to be paid.

(iii) Repayment was not to start for six years and would then continue until the year 2000.

(iv) If, in any year Great Britain had difficulties with its balance of payments, repayment could be waived that year and the repayment period extended by one year.

(b) The other terms were quite astounding. Great Britain had to agree:

(i) To make sterling freely convertible by July 1947.

(ii) To cease all trade discrimination and the sterling area to discontinue pooling its dollar resources.

(iii) To end exchange control within one year.

(iv) Not to use the loan to pay other creditors.

Clearly, the United States did not appreciate the seriousness of Great Britain's difficulties, and was too keen to return to "normal." However, only Clause 1—to make sterling convertible—was carried out.

The harsh terms of the Washington Agreement contrast strongly with the generous assistance given by the United States under the Marshall Plan.

THE CONVERTIBILITY CRISIS (1947)

3. Sterling becomes convertible. The convertibility crisis was the direct result of Great Britain's attempt to make sterling freely convertible under the Washington Loan agreement.

Although it had been expected that the American loan would last five years the credit was almost exhausted within eighteen months. The reasons for this were:

(a) Great Britain's need for imports was much greater than had been expected.

(b) The sharp rise in American prices (the result of undue haste in the relaxation of wartime controls) reduced the value of the loan in real terms.

In July 1947, as agreed, sterling became convertible.

4. Withdrawal of convertibility of sterling. Many other countries in addition to Great Britain were in difficulties as a result of the war, and the United States was the only country capable of exporting on a large scale. Consequently, advantage was quickly taken of the ability to exchange sterling for US dollars.

Convertibility had to be withdrawn after only five weeks to prevent Great Britain's gold and dollar reserves being completely exhausted.

5. Effects of the failure of convertibility.

(a) The inauguration of the Marshall Plan for American assistance to Europe, as a result of realisation by the United States of the difficulties facing the countries of Europe. During 1948-50 assistance to the value of $4,800 million under this scheme was given by the United States not only to former allies, but also to ex-enemies and neutrals.

(b) Indefinite suspension of the Bretton Woods scheme, with regional trading instead of world-wide multi-lateral trade and a continuance of exchange control.

REGIONALISM

6. The European Payments Union. The Marshall Plan was administered in Europe by the OEEC (the Organisation for European Economic Co-operation). It had two aims:

(a) To provide American assistance to Europe.

(b) To encourage multi-lateral trade among European nations.

To assist this second purpose the European Payments Union was established. This was, in effect, a regional version of the Bretton Woods scheme. It ceased operations in 1959, when most European currencies became convertible.

7. The sterling area.

(a) Before 1914. During this period Great Britain was the banking and financial centre for a large number of mainly undeveloped, dependent territories. The sterling area then comprised the British Empire.

(b) Between the two world wars. After the collapse of the gold standard in the 1930s many countries linked their currencies to sterling because they found it gave them greater stability. At this time the sterling area comprised the Commonwealth (except Canada), some European countries (including France), Argentina, Japan and many others.

(c) 1945–72. During these years the sterling area comprised the Commonwealth (except Canada) and a number of other countries which found it to their advantage to pool their gold and dollar resources.

In effect, the sterling area came to an end in 1972 when it came to be restricted to the United Kingdom, the Republic of Ireland, the Isle of Man, the Channel Islands and Gibraltar.

THE DEVALUATION OF STERLING (1949)

8. Causes of the devaluation

(a) Over-valuation of the pound in 1945. In 1945 it was impossible to value the pound precisely, a rate of $4.03 to the £ being chosen, and this over-valued sterling.

(b) The British balance of payments. Over-valuation of a currency produces a fundamental disequilibrium in a country's balance of payments. Not surprisingly, Great Britain had serious deficits in its balance of payments during the 1940s.

(c) American influence. The Americans believed that while countries were receiving assistance under the Marshall Plan they would never take the measures necessary to bring their balances of payments into balance. This view was strengthened by the cost of the Marshall Plan, and the fact that in 1948-49 the United States experienced its first post-war recession.

(d) The immediate cause. It was widely believed — especially in the United States — that Great Britain, whether it liked it or not, would be compelled to devalue the £. This led to foreign buyers of British goods postponing their purchases in the expectation of a fall in prices following devaluation. This widened still further the trade gap and made devaluation inevitable.

9. The theory of devaluation. The aim of devaluation as a remedy for a fundamental disequilibrium in the balance of payments is to bring the internal and external values of a currency into line:

(a) Devaluation reduces the prices of a country's exports and so stimulates the demand for them.

(b) Devaluation increases the prices of imports and so checks the demand for them.

Thus, payments on international account are reduced and receipts increased, thereby bringing the balance of payments into equilibrium.

10. The effects of devaluation.

(a) An increase in exports. The immediate effect was a large increase in exports due to:

(i) The backlog of unfulfilled orders.
(ii) The lower prices of British goods to foreign buyers.

(b) A rise in the prices of imports. The extent to which this will reduce imports depends on the elasticity of demand for imports. For example, British demand for imported raw materials is very inelastic. Thus, there occurs:

(i) A rise in the cost of living.
(ii) A rise in the cost of production of those British manufactures that are dependent on imported raw materials.

(c) A stimulus to inflation. The effectiveness of the devaluation of a currency, therefore, depends on the ability to keep down export prices. There should, therefore, be no increases in wages merely on account of higher internal prices due to devaluation. Proposals for a "wage freeze" received little support from the trade unions. Therefore, the ultimate effect of devaluation was a further stimulus to inflation. Thus, the advantages accruing to devaluatiuon were short-lived.

THE PROBLEM OF PERSISTENT INFLATION

11. Phases of inflation. Three phases of inflation can be distinguished:

(a) War-time inflation, 1938–45.
(b) Post-war inflation, 1945–49.
(c) Persistent inflation since 1949.

12. War-time inflation. Internal inflation has become a feature of all great wars:

(a) Government experience is too great to be financed by taxation and there has to be recourse to:

(i) Borrowing from the community (non-inflationary).
(ii) Borrowing from the banks } (inflationary).
(iii) Creation of money by the State } (inflationary).

(b) In spite of price controls wages increase while the production of consumers' goods falls.

13. The inflationary gap. This is the excess of Government expenditure over revenue from taxation, together with nonbank borrowing. It is most likely to arise in time of war, but is can also arise whenever a Government is reluctant to increase taxation sufficiently to cover its expenditure.

14. Post-war inflation. Inflation is often more severe in the post-war period than during the war itself:

(a) For a time consumers' goods are still in short supply.
(b) Demand for all kinds of consumers' goods is very great, especially for durable consumers' goods which have depreciated or become worn out during the war.
(c) Wages are high.
(d) People no longer wish to save. Instead they wish to spend money saved during the war.

15. Persistent inflation. After previous great wars, inflation spent itself in the post-war years. The inflation engendered by the Second World War was prolonged beyond the post-war period for a number of reasons:

(a) The devaluation of the £ (1949).
(b) The Korean war (1950–1):

(i) Many countries began stockpiling war materials.
(ii) Fear, especially in the United States, that it might be the beginning of another world war.
(iii) Re-armament.

(c) Government responsibility for full employment.
(d) Excessive capital investment—the attempt to do too much in too short a time.
(e) Efforts to increase the rate of economic growth.
(f) Increasing power and militancy of the trade unions.

GOVERNMENT POLICY (1945–51)

16. Cheap money. Adopted by the Government because of:

(a) Belief that Bank rate was ineffective.
(b) A low rate of interest reduces cost of borrowing to the Government and local authorities.

The attempt to introduce an ultra-cheap money policy failed when Government departments themselves had to take up most of a new issue of unredeemable $2\frac{1}{2}$ per cent Treasury stock.

17. Consequences of cheap money. Since Bank rate was not used, other instruments of policy had to be employed:

(a) Physical controls:

(i) Price controls.
(ii) Rationing of consumer goods.
(iii) Control of investment.
(iv) Licensing of building materials.
(v) Exchange controls.

(b) Fiscal policy. The budget was first used as an instrument of economic policy in 1947, the aim being to achieve a large surplus to reduce consumers' purchasing power.

18. Cheap money and inflation. Cheap money of itself tends to increase inflationary pressure. Physical controls only repress inflation, without getting rid of it. A budget surplus can be achieved only by higher taxation; higher indirect taxes raise prices and so lead to demands for higher wages.

CHAPTER XVI

RECENT MONETARY PROBLEMS

THE INTERNAL SITUATION:

FULL EMPLOYMENT AND INFLATION

As already seen, inflation after the Second World War was prolonged beyond the immediate post-war period for a number of reasons (*see* XV, **15**)

1. Government responsibility for full employment. To make certain of achieving this objective a government is likely to over-stimulate demand so that over-full employment results. This stimulates the inflationary spiral by increasing the bargaining power of the trade unions. Lord Beveridge declared that full employment without inflation was possible only if the trade unions were prepared to adopt a new attitude towards wages.

2. Unemployment. There are two aspects of unemployment:

(a) The level of employment. During the twelve years 1953–64 the number of unemployed exceeded the number of unfilled vacancies during most years. Over-full employment, therefore, occurred during these years. Over-full employment was associated with inflationary years, and when employment fell below this level it was the result of measures taken to check inflation. During 1973–75 unemployment increased very considerably, with fewer vacancies than the number unemployed.

(b) Distribution of unemployment. Unemployment, however has not been evenly spread over the country during these years. Throughout the period there was over-full employment in London, the South generally, the Midlands and East and West Yorkshire. On the other hand, full employment has not been reached even in the best years in the North-East, Scotland or South Wales.

3. "Stop-go" policy. This term was applied to alter nations of expansionary and deflationary policies.

(a) Inflation and full employment. The two aims *(i)* of checking inflation and *(ii)* maintaining full employment have proved to be impossible to reconcile.

To ensure that not less than full employment is achieved has required so high a level of demand that prices have risen and a shortage of labour has resulted, that is, over-full employment has occurred. This has been followed by increases in wages and further rises in prices. Most surprisingly the serious inflation of 1969–75 was accompanied by a steep rise in unemployment.

(b) Years of crisis. When measures have been taken to check inflation, unemployment has increased. A policy of disinflation has also often been made necessary by the external situation, sometimes the consequence of internal inflation and sometimes the result of external events. Thus, sterling crises requiring a disinflationary policy occurred in 1952, 1955, 1957, 1961, and 1964–67.

(c) Years of expansion. Once the difficulties were overcome, rising unemployment led to a reversal of policy, a removal of restrictions and an expansion of bank credit, so that an inflationary situation soon returned.

This policy was blamed for Great Britain's slow rate of economic growth during the 1950s and 1960s.

4. Productivity, wages and prices. If *real* wages are to be increased productivity must first be improved, and money wages must not be increased at a greater rate than the increase in productivity. Since 1945 wages have continued to increase at a much greater rate than productivity, especially since 1969. In consequence there has been a continuous rise in prices.

In 1970–73 a great effort was made to increase Great Britain's rate of economic growth, the ultimate aim being to make possible a rise in *real* wages.

5. Inflation in the 1970s. During the 1970s the rate of inflation in Great Britain increased at an alarming rate, the main causes being:

(a) Full employment, as already noted, had done much to keep the inflationary spiral in motion. The inflation of 1970–75, however, was accompanied by increasing unemployment.

(b) The militancy of the trade unions, especially in cases where strikes can dislocate social life, has increased the longer full employment has lasted. Whatever the economic conditions—boom or recession—the unions have come to expect wage increases of ever larger amounts and at more frequent intervals.

(c) The attempt to improve the rate of economic growth involved a large increase in consumers' demand. The consequent increase in imports gave a further powerful stimulus to inflation and, together with the rise in the prices of imported raw materials, itself the result of the rapid economic growth of many countries, produced a heavy deficit in the British balance of payments without much effect on this country's economic growth.

(d) Unbalanced budgets. These were an important cause of the acceleration of inflation in Great Britain in 1973–75, the excess of State expenditure over revenue being over £3,000 million in both 1973 and 1974 and over £12,000 million in 1975. The result was an increase in the money supply which doubled in the six years to 1975 (*see* **6** below).

(e) Floating exchange rates. These remove the brake on over-expansionist policies that gold provided. This foreign exchange system requires the monetary authorities to show great restraint, since with flexible exchange rates a country need never deflate.

(f) Inflation is a world-wide phenomenon. On this account it is very difficult for an individual country to keep inflation under control.

ATTEMPTS TO CONTROL INFLATION

6. Means adopted to fight inflation. Governments over the years have tried to control inflation by different means:

(a) Physical controls. After 1951 these were gradually removed, except exchange control, which was not seriously relaxed until 1959.

(b) Bank rate. As already noted, the use of Bank rate as an instrument of policy was revived in 1951 and it has continued to be used since then. Failure to check inflation by physical controls was the reason for its revival. During 1964–72 Bank rate only occasionally fell below 5 per cent and was generally between 6 per cent and 8 per cent and so this was a period of high interest rates, that is, of dear money.

(c) Fiscal policy. Throughout the period Bank rate was supplemented by fiscal policy, with deliberate budgeting for a surplus whenever it was necessary to check inflation. Since direct taxation acts as a disincentive to workers, to increase income tax would have an adverse effect on production. Thus, the increase had to be in indirect taxation and in the duties on alcoholic drink and tobacco. In 1962 the Chancellor obtained powers to vary these taxes by a limited extent—by Order in Council between budgets—the "regulator." However, by raising the prices of many commodities, the effect of such taxation can itself be inflationary.

More recently there has been an increase in direct taxation—income tax, corporation tax and capital gains tax.

(d) The "package deal." This term was applied by the *Radcliffe Report* (1959) to the use of a group of instruments of policy at the same time—Bank rate and fiscal policy combined with variations in hire-purchase regulations, the Treasury directive or special deposits.

It may be that each instrument of policy by itself had little effect, but employed together they were more effective, although the existence of other sources of credit, such as finance houses, industrial bankers, merchant banks, building societies, insurance companies (for very large borrowers) and possibly trade credit, makes the contraction of bank credit of less effect than formerly. Deposits in building societies are very similar to deposits on deposit account at commercial banks, largely comprising money held as a reserve for the precautionary motive.

The *Radcliffe Report* (1959) drew attention to these other sources of credit to which people will have recourse if bank lending is restricted. Consequently, when the Government wishes to restrict credit the Bank of England as its agent now not only makes this known to the commercial banks but also to these other financial intermediaries.

(e) The money supply. Some economists regard restriction of the money supply as the key to the control of inflation. It would require to be brought about gradually, for in the short run it would cause some unemployment, though perhaps not to as great an extent as might occur in very severe inflation.

7. Incomes policy. In an effort to check the inflationary spiral, governments have tried several times to introduce an incomes policy:

(a) The Council on Prices, Productivity and Incomes. This body was set up in 1957, its function being to report periodically on the relations between prices, productivity and incomes. The trade unions refused to accept its findings.

(b) The National Incomes Commission. This body was set up in 1962 in an attempt to establish an incomes policy by relating increases in wages to the rate of increase in productivity. Again there was strong opposition from the trade unions.

(c) The National Economic Development Council. Also established in 1962, its main function was to promote a measure of State planning of production in order to increase the rate of economic growth in Great Britain, but it was also asked to seek means of stabilising industrial incomes.

(d) An incomes policy, 1964–69. The Government, elected in 1964, persuaded the trade unions to agree in principle to an incomes policy (in return for increased taxation of profits and capital gains), a Prices and Incomes Board being established in 1965 to watch over increases in prices and wages. During 1965–68 the PIB's efforts to keep a check on prices and wages were fairly successful, but the devaluation of sterling in 1967 and the increasing opposition of the trade unions led to the abandonment of this policy and there followed grossly inflationary increases in wages during 1969–70.

(e) Revival of incomes policy 1973–74. Failure to prevent wages rising ahead of productivity led to the re-imposition of an incomes policy in 1973. This was abandoned in 1974 in favour of the "Social Contract"—voluntary wage restraint by agreement with the TUC.

THE EXTERNAL SITUATION: CONVERTIBILITY OF STERLING (1959)

8. Bretton Woods and convertibility.

(a) Advantages of convertibility:

(i) It is necessary for the full development of multi-lateral trade, since to reach its maximum, international trade must be multi-lateral.

(ii) It is a pre-requisite for sterling as an international currency.

(b) Disadvantage of convertibility: It deprives a country of complete control over its currency in times of crisis.

At Bretton Woods the advantages of convertibility appeared to outweigh the disadvantages, and so convertibility of currencies became an important feature of the scheme.

9. The failure to maintain convertibility, 1947. As noted in XV, **3–5**, sterling was made convertible in 1947, but after only five weeks convertibility had to be withdrawn.

(a) Causes of failure.

(i) The abnormal circumstances of the time.

(ii) The introduction of convertibility too soon after the conclusion of a great war.

(b) Effects of failure of convertibility. The main effect was to delay considerably the restoration of convertibility. Nearly twelve years elapsed before sterling was again made convertible in 1959.

10. Steps towards convertibility.

(a) The re-opening of the *foreign exchange market.* Sterling was permitted to fluctuate only between a rate of 2.78 and 2.82 dollars to the £.

(b) The re-opening of the *London gold market* in 1954.

(c) Regional convertibility, sterling being made convertible in each of three areas:

(i) The area of the American Account—the United States, Canada, Mexico.

(ii) The sterling area.

(iii) The rest of the world.

(d) Gradual *relaxation of exchange control regulations.*

(e) Non-resident convertibility. This was the status given to sterling in January 1959, that is, free convertibility to foreign holders of sterling, with limitation of the amount of foreign currency available to British people, mainly to prevent the export of capital for investment. After 1959 these restrictions were gradually relaxed.

STERLING CRISES

11. Internal influences. During the period 1951–65 there were several sterling crises—in 1952, 1955, 1957, 1961, 1964–67 and 1972.

Generally the deficit in the British balance of payments was the direct result of the internal situation. Fear of a recession turning into a serious depression led to excessive stimulus being given to the economy in order to restore full employment as quickly as possible. Inevitably the resulting expansion of demand brought about a return of inflation in the domestic sphere and a large increase in imports, both of raw materials and manufactured goods, with, as a result, a deficit in the balance of payments. During 1970–73 inflation was further stimulated by efforts to increase the rate of economic growth.

12. External influences.

(a) The revaluation of some currencies. A country with a strong currency will regularly have a credit balance in its balance of payments. This under-valuation of the currency will lead to its being revalued. This has occurred several times with the German Deutsche Mark and the Netherlands guilder. One of the immediate effects of the appreciation of other currencies is an outflow of funds from London.

(b) Sterling as an international currency. Difficulties with its balance of payments on current account are always worsened on capital account for Great Britain by an outflow of funds from the country—the result of sterling being an international currency and so being widely held. As such, sterling is subject to speculative capital movements.

(c) Export of capital. Increased investment abroad by British companies and, since the relaxation of exchange control in 1955, by individuals in Great Britain.

(d) Devaluation of sterling. In spite of efforts to check increases in incomes and prices, the devaluations of 1949 and 1967, after brief time-lags, had the effect of still further stimulating inflation.

13. Inadequacy of Great Britain's reserves. Great Britain's balance of payments problem was aggravated by the inadequacy of its reserves. In spite of the fall in the value of money the reserves were very little greater in the 1970s than in the 1960s. In consequence, a fall in the reserves became a more serious matter, the purpose of reserves being to enable a country to ride out the fluctuations in international trade that are bound to occur.

14. Measures taken to deal with sterling crises.

(a) Disinflationary measures. The aim was to curtail internal demand in order to check the demand for imports. This was generally achieved by a combination of monetary policy (including new instruments such as special deposits), fiscal policy and hire-purchase restrictions, known as the "package deal."

(b) Efforts to stimulate exports. These mainly took the form of Government exhortation, though increased assistance was given through the Exports Credit Guarantee Department, but in 1964 a rebate of that part of costs due to taxation was given to exporters.

15. Bank rate and the sterling crises. It remains a matter of controversy whether Bank rate was an effective instrument of monetary policy for the internal situation.

Faced with a sterling crisis a high Bank rate, if prompt action was taken and other measures adopted to curtail excessive internal demand, was generally effective in stemming an outflow of funds. Delay in raising Bank rate in 1964 made it slower to take effect.

THE DEVALUATION OF STERLING (1967)

16. Balance of payments difficulties 1964-67. The sterling crisis of 1964–67 was the longest and most serious of post-1951 crises. The main reasons for this were:

(a) The attempts at all costs to stimulate economic growth in 1963–64 brought about a huge deficit in the balance of payments on *current account.*

(b) Effective action to deal with the situation was not taken in time. As a result confidence in sterling declined and heavy withdrawals of sterling caused a large deficit on *capital account.*

17. Causes of the devaluation of sterling (1967).

(a) The changing value of sterling relative to other currencies. Inflation was a world-wide problem but it was more severe in the U.K. than in most other western countries.

(b) The exchange rate was permitted to fluctuate only within narrow limits. It was generally thought that this rate over-valued sterling.

(c) Sterling, like the U.S. dollar, was an international currency, but neither of these could meet the needs of expanding world trade. The U.K.'s reserves too were inadequate for sterling to play this role.

18. The attempt to avoid devaluation. Since the devaluation of a major currency can have world-wide repercussions, the I.M.F. and the Group of Ten (*see* **21** *(f)* below) assisted the U.K. by massive loans, but these proved to be of no avail. In terms of the U.S dollar sterling was devalued from 2.80 to 2.40, fluctuation being permitted between 2.38 and 2.42.

19. Effects of the 1967 devaluation. The general effects of devaluation of a currency as a means of correcting an adverse balance of payments have already been considered VII, **21**). (*See also* XV, **9, 10** for a discussion of the effects of the devaluation of sterling in 1949.)

(a) A substantial surplus in the balance of payments would be required for some years to repay the loans incurred in the attempt to avoid devaluation.

(b) The immediate effect was a rise in the prices of imported foodstuffs and raw materials. In time this would cause a rise in the cost of living and, with trade unions' growing impatience with an incomes policy, a further stimulus would be given to inflation. Eventually this wiped out the immediate advantages derived from devaluation.

(c) In 1949 most other currencies had been devalued in line with sterling, as all were weak at that time in relation to the U.S. dollar. In 1967, however, the only countries to devalue were those dependent on the U.K. as a market for their exports. There was no uniform policy even among members of the sterling area.

INTERNATIONAL LIQUIDITY

20. The International Monetary Fund. The framers of the constitution of the IMF recognised the necessity for providing assistance to a country in *temporary* difficulties with its balance of payments. To enable this to be done, the IMF was provided with a pool of gold and currencies of members according to the quotas assigned to them. These quotas determined members' drawing rights (*see* IX, **20**), which it was expected would be sufficient for the purpose for which they were intended. The huge increase since 1945 in the size of both deficits and surpluses in balances of payments rendered these drawing rights, in spite of two increases in members' quotas, inadequate in view of:

(a) the enormous expansion of the volume of international trade, and
(b) the continuing rise in prices.

21. International liquidity today.

(a) The gold and convertible currency reserves of each country, mainly gold (49 per cent of world monetary reserves).

(b) The U.S. dollar is now, after gold, the most important international means of payment. This has been helped by the introduction of Eurodollars, the use of which has enormously increased since 1960. These are claims to U.S. dollars held by banks and other financial institutions outside the United States. London is the main centre of the Eurodollar market (28 per cent).

(c) Sterling, for long an international currency, is no longer longer the principal one ($9\frac{1}{2}$ per cent).

(d) The drawing rights of each member of the IMF. The quotas—and, therefore, the drawing rights—were increased in 1959, 1965 and 1969. It became usual for a country which expected to exercise its drawing rights to negotiate a stand-by agreement with the IMF in advance.

(e) Special Drawing Rights (SDRs), issued by the IMF, were devised for the purpose of increasing international liquidity. The amount issued during the years 1970-74 was $3,500 million per year (50 per cent more than the IMF's ordinary drawing rights), each country's allotment being related to its quota under the IMF's constitution. SDRs are not to be regarded as loans but as permanent additions to members' reserves.

(f) Central bank co-operation:

(i) The Basle Arrangements. When there was a run on sterling in 1961, following the revaluation of the West German DM, eight European central banks met under the auspices of the Bank of International Settlements at Basle and a loan was made to Great Britain.

(ii) The "Group of Ten." This comprised ten countries, including Great Britain and the United States,* the central banks of which agreed to lend to the IMF whenever necessary to increase the Fund's resources.

To protect sterling, Great Britain had to seek international assistance in 1961 and 1964–67.

THE BREAKDOWN OF THE BRETTON WOODS SYSTEM

22. The IMF under strain. The Bretton Woods scheme had two essential features:

(a) currency values linked to gold (through the US dollar) with convertibility to gold.
(b) In general fixed exchange rates, though these could be changed in certain circumstances.

In course of time, with different rates of economic growth and different rates of inflation, internal values of currencies diverged more and more from the official exchange rates. The monetary crises of the 1960s were the consequence of this. A great strain, therefore, was placed on the IMF. The crisis of 1968 was resolved by the introduction of a two-tier price system for gold. By 1971, however, a number of countries had gone over to floating exchange rates. Then the United States declared itself to be no longer willing to buy and sell gold freely.

23. The Smithsonian Agreement. This agreement was the last attempt of the IMF to return to fixed exchange rates, a new set of parities being negotiated for the leading currencies. It lasted only six months.

24. The switch to "floating" rates. In June 1972, after huge speculative pressure, sterling was allowed to float. By January 1973 most of the world's leading currencies were being allowed to float.

A system of flexible exchange rates has the advantage of eliminating foreign exchange crises and a country's concern for its gold reserves. On this system it is never necessary to deflate, but the danger of hyperinflation is greatly increased. For example, during 1971–75 the pound sterling depreciated by 29 per cent in terms of other currencies (*see* Flexible Exchange

*The other eight are West Germany, France, Italy, the Netherlands, Belgium, Sweden, Canada, Japan.

Rates pp. 62-64). The huge increase in the price of oil in 1973–74 would have severely tested any system of foreign exchange.

25. Reform of the Bretton Woods system. Throughout 1972–74 committees of the IMF struggled hard to reform the system set up at Bretton Woods but failed to agree. It had been easier to reach agreement in 1944–45 when there were only two major currencies than in 1972–74 when no single nation dominated world trade.

INTERNATIONAL AID

26. Aid from individual countries. A feature of recent years has been the enormous assistance given to the developing countries of the world by those with developed economies.

This development grew out of American aid to Europe under the Marshall Plan (*see* XV, **8**) during the post-war period, when the United States was the only country capable of helping others on a large scale. During the decade 1955–65 American aid was increased and widened to such an extent that the United States, with a credit balance of payments on current account, found itself with a large deficit on capital account which was more than double its current surplus. In consequence it experienced a heavy outflow of gold.

In addition to the assistance given by the United States, aid to developing countries is also being given by Great Britain, France, Germany, the Netherlands, Russia, Canada, Australia and Japan.

27. Aid from international institutions. Aid usually takes the form of grants; from international institutions (except the FAO) it generally takes the form of loans.

International institutions providing aid in some form or other for developing nations include:

(*a*) *The Food and Agricultural Organisation* (FAO) of the United Nations.

(*b*) *The International Bank for Reconstruction and Development* (the World Bank), established under the Bretton Woods agreement of 1944 to provide loans, mainly to governments, for reconstruction or capital development.

(*c*) *The International Finance Corporation* (IFC), established in 1956 for the purpose of supplementing the activities of the World Bank by providing assistance to private enterprise in developing countries. (Now part of FFI.)

(d) The International Development Association (IDA), established in 1960 to help to promote the economic development of developing countries.

PROGRESS TEST 4

RECENT MONETARY DEVELOPMENTS

1. Why did Great Britain in 1945 find it necessary to borrow from abroad? (XV, **1**)
2. "The terms of the Washington loan (1945) were a mixture of leniency and harshness." Elucidate this statement. (XV, **2**)
3. What is meant by the convertibility of a currency? (XV, **3**)
4. Account for Great Britain's failure to maintain convertibility in 1947. (XV, **4, 5**)
5. What are the main changes that have taken place in *(a)* the composition, and *(b)* the functions of the sterling area during the present century? (XV, **7**)
6. What advantages may a country hope to gain by devaluing its currency? What are the drawbacks to devaluation? (XV, **9, 10**)
7. Why was sterling devalued in 1949? (XV, **8**)
8. "The ultimate effect of the devaluation of the £ in 1949 was merely to give a further fillip to inflation." Explain this statement. (XV, **10**)
9. What is the "inflationary gap"? (XV, **13**)
10. Why is inflation often more severe in a post-war period than during the war itself? (XV, **14**)
11. For what reasons has inflation after the Second World War tended to persist beyond the immediate post-war period? (XV, **15**)
12. What is meant by a cheap money policy? (XV, **16-18**)
13. What are "physical controls"? (XV, **16**)
14. What have been the main influences since 1945 on the level of employment? (XVI, **2**)
15. Consider the relationship between productivity, wages and prices. (XVI, **3**)
16. Account for the revival in 1951 of Bank rate as an instrument of policy. (XVI, **5**)
17. Show the purpose of fiscal policy when employed as an ancillary to monetary policy. (XVI, **5**)
18. What was the "package deal"? (XVI, **6**)
19. What do you understand by an "incomes policy"? Describe the efforts made since 1957 to introduce such a policy. (XVI, **7**)
20. Why did short periods of credit restriction alternate with short periods of credit expansion during 1955-65? (XVI, **3**)
21. What were the effects of failure to maintain convertibility of sterling in 1947? (XVI, **9**)
22. Describe the main stages by which convertibility of sterling was achieved in 1959. (XVI, **10**)

23. What was "non-resident convertibility"? (XVI, **10**)

24. Since 1951 there has been a number of sterling crises. What were the main causes of these crises? (XVI, **11-13**)

25. Why was sterling devalued in 1967? (XVI, **16-17**)

26. Account for the breakdown of the Bretton Woods system. (XVI, **22-25**)

27. Why do you think the Smithsonian Agreement was doomed to failure? (XVI, **23**)

28. On what lines might it be possible to reform the International Monetary Fund? (XVI, **20-21**)

29. Explain the meaning of the term "international liquidity." (XVI, **20**)

30. For what purpose was the Group of Ten formed? Name the principal members of the Group. (XVI, **21**)

Further Reading

J. L. Hanson: *Monetary Theory and Practice.* (For a more detailed treatment of the whole field.)

APPENDIX I

EXAMINATION TECHNIQUE

For all examinations there are certain basic rules that must be followed:

1. Read the question carefully. Before attempting any question read it through carefully and do not start to answer it until you are quite certain what the examiner requires. Though this may appear to be obvious it is, nevertheless, one of the most frequent causes of candidates wasting their time by answering questions not asked by the examiner. It is one of the main causes of low marks.

2. Arrange the points of your answer in logical order. In your answer bring out these points in clear, grammatical, concise language. When it is necessary to illustrate by examples make sure these are quoted in the most appropriate places. To carry out this rule effectively it is a good plan to make a rough summary before starting your answer.

3. Keep strictly to the question throughout your answer, avoiding all irrelevant matter. The precise question asked by the examiner is the one—and only one—to be answered. Do not be tempted, as so many examinees are, to use a question merely to show off your knowledge of other parts of the subject, as you will earn no credit for this.

4. Apportion your time. Where each question carries equal marks, divide your time as nearly as possible equally among them.

Every subject of study, however, has its own examination technique.

5. Questions on monetary theory. These are of three main types:

(a) The question requiring a straightforward description of some monetary institution or theory.

(b) The question that requires the candidate to make use of his knowledge to compare or contrast two things, or to assess the importance of something.

(c) To discuss a quoted statement which is usually a half-truth, almost but hardly ever wholly right or wrong.

To many students, one of the particular difficulties of monetary questions is that the subject matter is developing all the time, and in more advanced examinations candidates are expected to be aware of the latest developments—very often too recent to have found a place in even the most recently published textbooks. For example, a textbook published late in 1971 would have been inadequate for an answer to a question on Bank rate at an examination in 1972. Again, a textbook published before 1956 might have correctly stated that during this century Great Britain had always had a deficit in its visible balance of trade, although in 1956 it had a credit balance of trade. There is only one way to overcome this difficulty, namely to keep abreast of present-day developments by reading *The Economist* and as many as possible of the current issues of the quarterly journals of the Bank of England, the commercial banks and the International Monetary Fund.

A model answer

Question. What instruments are available to a government at the present day to influence the level of economic activity? Consider the efficacy of these instruments.

Answer. The British government has made itself responsible for the maintenance of full employment. It aims to achieve this objective without serious inflation. Thus, if unemployment begins to increase, measures will have to be taken to stimulate economic activity in order to restore full employment. If, however, the economy is becoming overloaded and there is a danger of excessive inflation, it will be necessary for the government to check this tendency.

The traditional instruments of monetary policy employed by the Bank of England during the nineteenth and early twentieth centuries were Bank rate and open-market operations. This was the period of the gold standard, and the policy of the central bank at that time was not directed so much to influencing the level of economic activity as to protecting the country's gold reserves. To check an outflow of gold, Bank rate would be raised and the Bank of England would sell securities in the open market in order to reduce the cash reserves of the commercial banks and so compel them to restrict credit in order to reduce their total deposits. This deflationary policy would tend to check economic activity. In the case of an inflow of gold the reverse policy would be adopted, Bank rate being reduced and the Bank of England buying securities in the open market in order to increase the cash reserves of the commercial banks, thereby making it possible for them to increase their lending to businessmen and so bring about an expansion of economic activity.

The Bank of England always regarded Bank rate as its main instrument of policy, open-market operations being undertaken, as it was said, only to make bank rate "effective." The efficacy of open-market operations depends on the maintenance of a cash ratio by the commercial banks. If such banks possess "excess liquidity," open-market operations will be less effective. It has been argued, however, that without the assistance of open-market operations Bank rate would have had little effect, since they compel the commercial banks to take action, whereas the higher rate of interest may not deter a borrower if the future outlook for business appears bright to him. Against both instruments it can be said that they appear to be more effective in checking expansion, since in this case the effect of open-market operations is certain, whereas when the aim to stimulate expansion they merely make conditions more favourable to borrowers, who will still be unwilling to borrow if they take a pessimistic view of the future.

During the past 25 years a number of new instruments of policy have been tried. From the end of the Second World War until the early 1950s the problem was solely one of trying to keep inflation in check. For some years physical controls, such as price controls, rationing, licensing of raw materials, etc., imposed during the Second World War were continued. Coupled with a policy of "cheap money," these controls merely suppressed inflation without getting rid of it.

The failure of physical controls to contain inflation led to suggestions that fiscal policy should be tried. In the 1930s, when the problem was one of severe unemployment, it had been suggested that demand should be stimulated by deliberately budgeting for a deficit. In 1948, in conditions of inflation, it was proposed to remove the excess of purchasing power by budgeting for a large surplus, fiscal policy continuing to be accompanied by physical controls.

As the government found it difficult to curtail its expenditure a large budget surplus could be achieved only by increased taxation. Since direct taxation acts as a disincentive, it was indirect taxes, such as purchase tax and the duties on petrol, tobacco and alcoholic drink that had to be increased, the effect being a rise in the cost of living, and consequently by demands in the trade unions for higher wages. Thus in practice the budget surplus itself proved to be inflationary.

By 1951 it seemed clear to many people that the alternatives to monetary policy had proved to be ineffective. it was for this reason that Bank rate was revived in 1951 as an instrument of policy and physical controls gradually relaxed. The rise in Bank rate was accompanied by Treasury directives to the banks, first of a qualitative kind to restrict their lending to projects in the "national interest" (a difficult question for an individual banker to resolve), and later of a quantitative kind to reduce total bank lending, whatever might be the purpose of the loans. Fiscal policy continued to be employed, not so much for the sake of achieving a budget surplus as to check or stimulate, as the case might be, consumers' demand through changes in purchase tax. Fiscal policy was reinforced by variations in hire-purchase regulations, increasing or decreasing the amount of the initial deposit and the length of the period of repayment, to check or stimulate consumers' demand. In 1960, instead of the Treasury directive, the Bank of England asked the commercial banks for "special deposits" (at first 1 per cent and later 2 per cent of their total deposits) in order to reduce their cash basis and thereby reduce their lending. There was again a request for special deposits in 1965. Special deposits were similar in effect to open-market operations.

Thus, a group of instruments came to be employed together, the so-called "package deal," comprising Bank rate, fiscal policy, hire-purchase controls and the Treasury directive or special deposits. Taken as a whole the package deal appears to have been effective in achieving its purpose of checking demand in 1955-56 and 1960-62 and, perhaps more important, of stimulating demand and restoring full employment in 1958-59 and 1963-64.

How effective was each individual instrument of policy it is not easy to determine. Changes in purchase tax had directional effects, output in the industries concerned being definitely checked by an increase in tax and stimulated by a reduction in tax. Changes in hire-purchase regulations appear to have had similar effects. On account of their physical consequences the quantitative Treasury directive and special deposits appear to have been effective, though the efficacy of the latter depends on the banks' not having "excess reserves." It is much more difficult, however, to decide the extent to which Bank rate was effective, as it was never employed by itself, always forming part of a package deal. A 7 per cent Bank rate, however, appeared to be generally effective in a sterling crisis if raised to that level in time. The main criticism of the use of the package deal was that there was a tendency for the authorities to persist in a particular policy for too long, so that in the end a sharp reversal of policy was required.

APPENDIX II

TEST PAPERS

Treat these tests as examination papers after you have completed your study and carried out a thorough revision, and work them under strict examination conditions. If you find that you cannot answer the questions in Test 1 without reference to textbooks or journals carry out a further revision of the subject before attempting Test 2.

TEST 1

Answer FOUR questions only.

All questions carry equal marks.

Time allowed — 3 hours.

1. What are the main drawbacks to a fall in the value of money? Are there any benefits to be derived from such an occurrence?
2. Assess the importance of the "liquidity rules" of the English commercial banks.
3. Account for the difficulties experienced by Great Britain since 1945 with its balance of payments.
4. Describe the work of the International Monetary Fund and show how it ran into difficulties in the 1970s.
5. Of what importance is the distinction made in the budget between "above the line" and "below the line" revenue and expenditure?
6. Write brief notes on two of the following:
   (a) The velocity of circulation.
   (b) The terms of trade.
   (c) The Purchasing Power Parity Theory.
   (d) Central bank co-operation.

TEST 2

Answer FOUR questions only.

All questions carry equal marks.

Time allowed — 3 hours.

1. Of what importance are the dynamic functions of money to a modern economy?
2. "A commercial bank can lend only what has been deposited with it." Discuss this statement.
3. Consider the various means that have been adopted since 1951 *(a)* to check inflation, *(b)* to overcome difficulties with the balance of payments.
4. Assess the importance of the London money market to the British banking system at the present day.
5. Compare the economic effects of direct and indirect taxation.

6. Write brief notes on two of the following:
   (a) The legal restriction of the fiduciary issue.
   (b) "Floating" exchange rates.
   (c) "Stop-go" policy.
   (d) The International Bank.

APPENDIX III

SOME ABBREVIATIONS USEFUL TO STUDENTS OF MONETARY THEORY

B/E	Bill of exchange
BIS	Bank for International Settlements
EEC	European Economic Community
EFTA	European Free Trade Area
EIB	European Investment Bank
EPU	European Payments Union
FAO	Food and Agricultural Organisation
FCI	Finance Corporation for Industry
FFI	Finance for Industry
GATT	General Agreement on Tariffs and Trade
GNP	Gross National Product
HP	Hire-purchase
IB (or IBRD)	International (World) Bank (for Reconstruction and Development)
ICFC	Industrial and Commercial Finance Corporation
IDA	International Development Association
IFC	International Finance Corporation
IMF	International Monetary Fund
ITO	International Trade Organisation
NDC	National Debt Commissioners
NEDC	National Economic Development Council
NNP	Net National Product
OECD	Organisation for Economic Co-operation and Development
OEEC	Organisation for European Economic Co-operation
OFC	Overseas Food Corporation
OTC	Overseas Trading Corporation
PAYE	Pay as you earn
PIB	Prices and Incomes Board
SCIT	Special Commissioners of Income Tax
Stg	Sterling
TDR	Tax Deposit Receipt
TT	Telegraphic Transfer
VAT	Value added tax

INDEX